The Secret Chamber *of* Osiris

"In *The Secret Chamber of Osiris,* Scott Creighton presents an intriguing and insightful perspective on the Egyptian pyramids, the geometry of their placement, and their relationship to a body of ancient hidden knowledge. He succeeds in presenting well-considered ideas within the context of a very readable book."

LAIRD SCRANTON, AUTHOR OF
SACRED SYMBOLS OF THE DOGON:
THE KEY TO ADVANCED SCIENCE IN THE
ANCIENT EGYPTIAN HIEROGLYPHS

"Creighton exposes very real scientific problems and guides us along a fascinating path as he researches novel solutions and offers a radical and fresh explanation for one of the world's oldest mysteries. Scott's power of imagination is matched only by the discipline of his logic."

RAND FLEM-ATH, COAUTHOR OF
ATLANTIS BENEATH THE ICE:
THE FATE OF THE LOST CONTINENT

Praise for
Scott Creighton's *The Giza Prophecy*

"Remarkable . . . original . . . convincing . . . explosive."

GRAHAM HANCOCK, AUTHOR OF
FINGERPRINTS OF THE GODS

The
Secret Chamber
of Osiris

Lost Knowledge
of the
Sixteen Pyramids

SCOTT CREIGHTON

Bear & Company
Rochester, Vermont • Toronto, Canada

Bear & Company
One Park Street
Rochester, Vermont 05767
www.BearandCompanyBooks.com

Text stock is SFI certified

Bear & Company is a division of Inner Traditions International

Library of Congress Cataloging-in-Publication Data
Creighton, Scott.
  The secret chamber of Osiris : lost knowledge of the sixteen pyramids / Scott
Creighton.
        pages cm
  Summary: "Reveals the true purpose behind the pyramids of Giza and the
location of the secret vault of Egyptian treasures hidden on the Giza plateau."
Provided by publisher.
  Includes bibliographical references and index.
  ISBN 978-1-59143-769-7 (pbk.) — ISBN 978-1-59143-187-9 (e-book)
  1. Osiris (Egyptian deity) 2. Egypt—Religion. 3. Mythology, Egyptian. 4.
Pyramids of Giza (Egypt) 5. Egypt—Antiquities. I. Title.
  BL2450.O7C74 2014
  932'.01—dc23
                                                                    2014021617

Printed and bound in the United States by Lake Book Manufacturing, Inc.
The text stock is SFI certified. The Sustainable Forestry Initiative® program
promotes sustainable forest management.

10 9 8 7 6 5 4 3 2 1

Text design by Debbie Glogover and layout by Priscilla Baker
This book was typeset in Garamond Premier Pro with Galliard and Gill Sans used
as display typefaces

To send correspondence to the author of this book, mail a first-class letter to the
author c/o Inner Traditions • Bear & Company, One Park Street, Rochester, VT
05767, and we will forward the communication, or contact the author directly at
www.scottcreighton.co.uk.

*To my wife, Louise, whose generous, patient,
and warmhearted nature allowed me the
time and space to write this book;
and to my children, Jamie and Nina,
for even more of your marvelous questions—
for questions truly are more important
than answers. Love you all forever.*

"One day the Nile will rise and cover all Egypt with water, and drown the whole country." —*Ancient Egyptian* Book of the Dead

Contents

Foreword

Does the sophisticated positioning of the Giza pyramid complex point to a reservoir of knowledge hidden beneath the sand? This is the compelling question raised by Scott Creighton in *The Secret Chamber of Osiris*. Boldly tackling a puzzling series of inconsistencies in the record, he questions why the architects of these iconic monuments not only took on the great challenge of aligning them with north, south, east, and west but also considerably increased the difficulty of their task by including features that only appear to be functional during a solstice or equinox. In answering the questions he reveals something extraordinary subtly concealed within the very design of the complex.

Egyptologists tell us that the Giza pyramids were constructed to serve the pharaohs' vainglory. Scott finds this hypothesis preposterous, writing, "There are simply too many anomalies, too many affronts to common sense, too many facts that simply do not fit the tomb paradigm that is so embraced by the Egyptologists." He exposes very real scientific problems and guides us along a fascinating path as he researches novel solutions and offers a radical and fresh explanation for one of the world's oldest mysteries.

He suggests that the people of ancient Egypt were privy to a deep and largely forgotten secret: that the Earth experiences periodic catastrophes that destroy civilization. To arm themselves against such future events, they constructed pyramids—not as tombs, but rather as reservoirs that would preserve the building blocks of civilization. These caches contained not only precious information on how best to reboot civilization but also held a sufficient store of grains to sustain the survivors as they launched their daunting task.

In *The Atlantis Blueprint,* coauthor Colin Wilson and I propose that the underlying geometry of the Giza site can be used to pinpoint the location of Thoth's Holy Chamber (containing records from a lost civilization). Scott takes the same broad approach but concludes that a different geometric solution provides the answer. He offers good reasons to believe that Egyptian authorities are fencing off the exact location that he believes should be the focus of an excavation. These efforts include "CCTV, infrared sensors, motion detectors" as well as "metal detectors"—useful tools to keep any but the most official investigators well away from the site.

That an amateur archaeologist might be the inspiration for present-day excavations in Egypt is not as unexpected as we might think. Albert Einstein said, "You cannot solve a problem from the same consciousness that created it. You must learn to see the world anew."[1] Seeing ancient Egypt anew is precisely what Scott Creighton has done in *The Secret Chamber of Osiris.*

This engrossing book reminds us that geology, archaeology, and Egyptology were once the subjects of great minds. In the nineteenth century these disciplines were at the cutting edge of science. But in recent times our best minds have been drawn to engineering, physics, the digital sciences, and the biological revolution in all its myriad and nascent branches. The stagnation in the official branches of geology, archaeology, and Egyptology has given rise to a generation of independent researchers motivated above all by curiosity, the real driving force of science. They are not willing to accept a prevailing paradigm just because academia decrees it so.

The problems that Scott confronts are worthy of serious consideration from our new generation of informed investigators, whose tools include an understanding of astronomy, survey and construction techniques, geometry, world mythology, and plain old common sense—all skills frequently lacking among present-day Egyptologists.

Critical questions raised by Scott include: Why are there so few inscriptions found within the Giza pyramids? What was the purpose of incorporating massive granite blocks within the Great Pyramid? Why did the builders leave in place a pulley system that allowed entry to the so-called King's Chamber? Why not seal the entry for eternity? Scott writes, "One has to conclude that the ancient architects went out of their way to ensure that the Great Pyramid (and its internal chambers), although reasonably secure, was in no way as tightly secure as the builders *could* have made it: it is almost as though the builders were going out of their way to *invite* relatively easy access to whatever lay within" (italics added). If this statement doesn't pique your curiosity, nothing will!

Scott also takes us deep inside the mysterious motives of Colonel Richard William Howard Vyse, whose dubious discoveries set the compass for much of which is still taken as gospel by Egyptologists. Not only does Scott reveal new facts about the case, he also suggests a relatively simple empirical test that could once and for all determine Howard Vyse's veracity. Chapter 6, "Gunpowder and Plot," is a welcome addition to the cause of keeping the field honest.

Having spent decades trying to unravel the mysteries of the termination of the last ice age, I find that "Ages of Deluge and Drought" is a chapter that tackles subjects close to my heart. Although our conclusions differ somewhat, Scott has done a thorough job in articulating the problem. The point where we concur is important: the ancient Egyptians believed in cyclical time, which suggested to them that deluges that occurred in the past would inevitably be echoed in the future. And we both maintain that traditional geological explanations are incapable of resolving the mystery of the relatively rapid changes in ocean levels exhibited at the termination of the Pleistocene, not to mention the phenomena of massive extinctions and migrations of people across the globe. We both explain worldwide myths that depict a great flood, falling skies, and stars that appeared to change position as the fearful legacy of ancient people who suffered a terrible catastrophe.

For those curious about the ever-intriguing mystery of how the ancient Egyptian builders manipulated the massive stones used in the construction of the pyramids, the author presents a novel and fascinating solution—one that has hitherto been missed.

Scott's power of imagination is matched only by the discipline of his logic. He is not afraid of the difficult questions nor is he shy in admitting the lure of the mysterious. "The most beautiful thing we can experience is the mysterious. It is the source of all true art and all science," said Einstein. "He to whom this emotion is a stranger, who can no longer pause to wonder and stand rapt in awe, is as good as dead: his eyes are closed."[2] Scott's eyes are most definitely wide open!

RAND FLEM-ATH

RAND FLEM-ATH is a Canadian writer, librarian, and independent scholar. He has coauthored several books with his wife, writer Rose Flem-Ath—*When the Sky Fell: In Search of Atlantis* and *Atlantis Beneath the Ice*—and also with British writer Colin Wilson for *The Atlantis Blueprint*. He lives in British Columbia, Canada.

Acknowledgments

This book would not have been possible without the input, assistance, and encouragement of many individuals. I would first like to express my sincere thanks to everyone on the team at Inner Traditions • Bear & Company, whose professionalism took much of the pain out of producing this book.

To my nephew, Jim Buchanan, and my dear friends George Cummings, John Paul Servadei, and Shirley Gray—you have listened to my theories now for more years than any of us probably care to remember and have always done so with grace, good humor, and the odd provocative question. My lifelong friend Eric Watson, who sadly and unexpectedly departed this world for pastures new, would have been proud of you. Thank you all for your unstinting support over the years; it is appreciated more than you can possibly ever imagine.

Special mention must be made here also to John Ferguson, whose invaluable expertise and advice greatly assisted with some technical aspects of this book. Also to Dr Patricia Usick of the British Museum for arranging access to the Hill facsimiles and to Roger Bettridge and the staff of the Centre for Buckinghamshire Studies for providing access to the Howard Vyse archive. The Archive Department staff at the Mitchell Library, Glasgow, also deserves recognition for its generous and expert assistance in transcribing parts of the Howard Vyse journal.

My gratitude is also given to Sam Petry, Dennis Payne, and Audrey

Mulertt, who each, in his or her own unique and subtle way, assisted me greatly in the development of this book.

And finally, I could not, in all sincerity, complete these acknowledgments without mentioning the Monday-night gang of Andrew, Kenny and Louise, Sarah, Tony and Trisha, and last, but by no means least, Colin; thank you all so much for keeping me mostly sane throughout the course of this endeavor. I couldn't have done it without the craic and, of course, the beers.

Introduction

For the best part of two hundred years it has been the settled opinion among Egyptologists and other scholars that the great pyramid-building age of ancient Egypt served one purpose and one purpose alone: to construct for the god-kings of the ancient Egyptian people a monumental pyramid that would serve both as tomb and as the vehicle by which the king's soul could be transfigured and sent onward to take its place in the afterlife among the stars (the gods) of the heavens.

While this view of these first pyramids presently remains the prevailing opinion among many as being the original and true function of these structures, there is a growing body of compelling evidence that suggests this view to be quite erroneous and says that these great structures, rather than serving as "revivication instruments" for the kings, actually were intended and served as revivication instruments for the *kingdom.* In short, each of the first sixteen or so pyramids built in ancient Egypt was built as an *ark,* and collectively these early, giant pyramids represent the ark of the ancient Egyptian gods Osiris and Thoth—the *ark of the gods.*

To support its controversial conclusions, this book presents a broad array of evidence from many diverse sources and, with meticulous attention to detail, demonstrates precisely where conventional Egyptology has gone awry in its interpretation of this evidence and in its understanding of these magnificent, awe-inspiring monuments. *The Secret Chamber of Osiris* will show that there is a perfectly reasonable and viable alternative function for these monuments and, furthermore, that this alternative function resides within an equally valid ancient Egyptian cultural narrative.

The Secret Chamber of Osiris will show—with compelling evidence—how the first sixteen pyramids built in ancient Egypt were perceived as and would come to represent the allegorical "dismembered body of Osiris," the ancient Egyptian god of agriculture and rebirth, and that through the agency of Osiris it was hoped that the *kingdom* could be reborn after an anticipated cataclysm—the great deluge of Thoth.

Explaining the legendary *myth of Osiris* and how it speaks of a lost or hidden part of Osiris—a secret or hidden chamber—that may lie under the sands to the southwest of the Giza plateau, the book will take the reader on a vicarious journey of discovery to explore this possibility and, in so doing, will reveal some provocative new perspectives and answers to some of the enduring mysteries of ancient Egypt, mysteries that persist even to this day and that the prevailing mainstream paradigm fails to adequately answer.

As well as presenting many new and original ideas, *The Secret Chamber of Osiris* also revisits some old questions with fresh new evidence that is sure to reopen and reignite these old controversies. In particular the long-standing controversial claim of forgery having occurred within the Great Pyramid, first penned by international bestselling author Zecharia Sitchin, is revisited with new evidence that paints the character of Colonel Richard William Howard Vyse, the man who allegedly discovered ancient Egyptian hieroglyphic inscriptions within sealed chambers of the Great Pyramid in 1837, in a very different and questionable light.

While the primary focus of *The Secret Chamber of Osiris* concerns itself with the *why* question, that is, *why* the giant pyramids of ancient

Egypt were built, some time is taken within the book to also consider the *how* question, presenting an intriguing and somewhat radical new theory—supported by tangible evidence—as to *how* these structures might actually have been built.

The Secret Chamber of Osiris concludes with a truly startling revelation related to the quest to discover the legendary secret chamber of Osiris, showing how the theorized location of this hidden chamber—a location at Giza that had never before been explored—suddenly became the site of a major excavation by the Egyptian authorities shortly after I revealed the possible location of this secret chamber to the world.

This book is about collating the available evidence, discovering new evidence, and evaluating *all* the evidence in order to present a solid, well-grounded, no-nonsense alternative view to the mainstream opinion as to why our ancient ancestors expended so much blood, sweat, and tears into the construction of these giant monuments. In short, this book offers a new contextual paradigm—a *new Egyptology*—through which this remarkable civilization can be understood.

This is *The Secret Chamber of Osiris.*

1

Legends of Secret Chambers

The greatest obstacle to discovery is not ignorance—it is the illusion of knowledge.

DANIEL J. BOORSTIN,
PULITZER PRIZE–WINNING HISTORIAN
AND FORMER LIBRARIAN OF THE U.S. CONGRESS

CAIRO, MARCH 22, 2008, 11:30 A.M.

The hotel lobby was abuzz with tourists from just about every conceivable corner of the globe, most clustered in small groups, chatting avidly about their excursions from the previous day: up to Alexandria, down to Karnak, or over to the Great Pyramid at Giza. It was impossible not to find yourself affected by the sheer sense of expectation and excitement rising from their collective voice as the next exhilarating chapter of their Egyptian adventure was about to unfold: the Sphinx, a Nile cruise, the Museum of Egyptian Antiquities in Cairo, the Valley of the Kings. Or a thousand and one other marvels this ancient country has to offer.

Without doubt, however, not one of them would be embarking on the little adventure I had planned for myself that day—a seven-kilometer round-trip into the fringes of the western Egyptian desert, far from the throngs of bustling, chattering tourists that flocked in endless streams to absorb the delights of Egypt's more obvious attractions.

This was the start of an adventure that had, by this time, been over two years in the making, an adventure that had begun with a simple idea, a fleeting moment of inspired thought that had been burning in my mind from that first moment of epiphany some years back to my presence now in Egypt. And the thought that I was now here at Giza in the shadow of the great pyramids to pursue my curiosity brought with it a near permanent broad smile to my face, and more often than not this had others looking at me quizzically, wondering what secret lay behind my barely concealed excitement. One or two people I'd been chatting with at breakfast that morning had asked of my plans for the day, and I had simply told them that I'd be going on a long walk of discovery. This was all perfectly true, although the "discovery" part remained to be seen. I could sense, though, from their polite questioning, that they knew I was not being entirely open with them. The simple fact was, I couldn't be. Not yet; it was much too early.

After a few minutes impatiently pacing back and forth around the foyer, I was approached by the hotel concierge, who told me that my taxi was waiting outside. This was it; my quest to discover the legendary chamber of Osiris had finally begun. I quickly gathered my belongings from the lobby floor—backpack, the obligatory hat, and camera—and hurried through the sliding doors out into the blazing sunshine. Even this early in the day and year, Giza's climate was far from kind to a fair-skinned Scotsman more used to battling through sheets of horizontal rain than sweltering under a vertical wall of searing heat. For sure, before the day was out, I would be slapping on the sunblock aplenty and using every fluid ounce of water I had packed.

Before climbing into the taxi I made one final check inside my backpack, double-checking that everything was there—water, sunblock,

Ordnance Survey maps, compass, pedometer, and, of course, the small, granite pyramid "capstone" I had carried with me all the way from my home in Scotland to Giza—my very own "philosopher's stone," my "gift to Osiris."

Finding everything in order, I clambered into the beat-up taxi and gave the driver my destination—the amphitheater at Giza. Unsurprisingly, he didn't seem to understand my broad Scottish brogue. And speaking little to zero Egyptian Arabic, I took the backpack and pulled out a map, held it up, and pointed to the open-air theater that stood just to the west of the pyramid of Khafre (*Chephren* in Greek), the second largest of the Giza pyramids (although it actually appears larger than Khufu's Great Pyramid as a result of it having been built on the central, high ground of the plateau).

The driver squinted his eyes at the map, shook his head, and spoke in broken English. "No theater. Gone. Theater closed."

"Yes, I know it's closed," I said, nodding reassuringly. "Theater please." I tapped a finger on the map a couple of times, as if this would somehow convey to the driver that I knew what I was doing, even if he didn't. He casually shrugged his shoulders, muttered something in Arabic, puffed on his cigarette, slipped the car into gear, and we set off.

I had traveled by bus and taxi a number of times by then in and around Cairo and had come to learn that each new experience would surely be no less hair-raising than all the others. Taxis, buses, trucks, horses with carts, and donkeys all shared the same highway, and it didn't seem to perturb any of them how slow or fast they traveled; there didn't seem to be a speed limit. Vehicles had indicators, but these were rarely, if ever, used. By far the "indicator" of choice was the car horn, thousands of them beeping and blasting in a cacophony of noise at anything that came too close or insisted in squeezing past. Buses and trucks casually drifted across lanes toward each other almost at will and would have made a taxi sandwich of us on a number of occasions but for the sharp braking or accelerating of my driver who, after a few sharp blasts on his own car horn, was otherwise underwhelmed by it, seemed to take it all in his stride—a typical day at the office. I lost count of the number of times I found myself gnawing on a knuckle as some pedestrian stepped straight out into the oncoming traffic, hand aloft like a police traffic controller in order to get himself across the busy road.

I'd been in the taxi no more than ten minutes when, in the distance, a great geometrical shape suddenly appeared on the horizon, towering high above the urban sprawl of houses, shops, high-rise apartment buildings, and construction cranes: the Great Pyramid of Khufu at Giza, known to Egyptologists simply as G1. It was hard to imagine that thousands of years ago this entire area—but for the pyramid site itself—would have been nothing but remote and empty desert for as far as the eye could see. The main method of transportation in ancient times wouldn't have been by motor vehicle on bustling, crazy highways but rather by boat along the banks of the great River Nile, the main artery and lifeblood of the country. Egypt truly was, as the Greek historian Herodotus had written more than two millennia ago, the "Gift of the Nile," for without this great waterway irrigating and fertilizing the Nile Valley for thousands of miles, Egypt simply could never and would never have existed.

Seeing the Great Pyramid looming large on the horizon brought back memories of my first visit to this magnificent monument some two days earlier on the spring equinox, when, in the company of world-renowned alternative historians and authors Graham Hancock and Robert Bauval, I stood in humble, reverent silence between the paws of the Sphinx, watching the equinoctial sunrise. At this special time of year at Giza the eternal gaze of the Sphinx is fixed due east, directly on the disc of the sun as it begins to peep over the eastern horizon—truly a spectacular sight to behold (see figure 1.1 on page 8).

As the blazing golden orb of the sun gradually emerged ahead, behind us the last flicker of a glorious silver moon was sinking in the west beyond the darkened silhouette of Khafre's majestic pyramid, these wondrous, celestial mechanics drawing gasps of fascination and delight from a few other hardy souls who had ventured out that early,

Photo: Scott Creighton

Figure 1.1. The Sphinx greets the dawn.

chilly March morning to bear witness to this unique and awe-inspiring spectacle.

Thirty minutes or so later the entire Giza plateau was tinged with golden-orange hues from the newly risen sun, and farther up the plateau in the distance the eastern flanks of the three giant pyramids were burning a fiery red, just as they had done for thousands of years. From my vantage point at the rear of the Sphinx enclosure I had a grand view of all three of the main pyramids, although the base of the Great Pyramid was partially obscured here by the rise of the plateau. With these three giant geometric shapes thrusting up from the desert sands into a cloudless sky, it was truly surreal, a landscape that seemed more like something from the movie *2001: A Space Odyssey* than something created from the hands of an ancient people who had lived thousands of years earlier at the dawn of history.

From this distance the triangular form of the pyramids appeared quite perfect, the ragged edges of the layers upon layers of stacked limestone blocks barely perceptible. The outer casing stones of white Tura limestone that had once made the pyramid's sides perfectly smooth (rather than their current stepped appearance) had long since vanished after an earthquake in medieval times had apparently loosened them, bringing them crashing to the ground, whereupon the grateful citizens of Cairo quarried them for various new buildings and monuments around the ancient city. Today at Giza only the uppermost section of Khafre's Pyramid and the bases of Khufu's and Menkaure's Pyramids still present some of these smooth outer casing stones.

My objective that first morning had been to visit the Great Pyramid, which Egyptologists have attributed to Khufu (*Cheops* in Greek), the second king of the Fourth Dynasty of ancient Egypt, who, according to Egyptologists, lived circa 2,550 BCE. I had a very particular reason for wanting to visit the Great Pyramid and especially so at this special time of the year, at sunrise during the spring (vernal) equinox.

In the company of Bauval, I trudged up the sloping plateau in the direction of Khafre's Pyramid, roughly following the line of the great causeway that had once run from the Valley and Sphinx Temples (which, in ancient times, would have graced a small harbor on the banks of the Nile) up to the ruins of the so-called Mortuary Temple, which had once stood on the east face of the pyramid. Something about this placement of Khafre's Pyramid on the plateau had always puzzled me; I turned to Bauval.

"Robert," I began as we walked together up the gentle slope of the plateau toward the middle pyramid of Khafre, "if Khufu was the first king to build a pyramid here on the plateau, why did he not choose for himself the high, central ground where Khafre built his pyramid? Why did Khufu opt to build his pyramid over on the lower ground at the very edge of the plateau? Surely if Khufu was the first king to build a pyramid here at Giza he would have chosen the high, central ground of the plateau. By doing that he could have ensured that no future king would have been able to surpass his achievement. Why didn't Khufu build his pyramid on the high ground of the plateau?"

With his customary enigmatic smile, Bauval replied simply, "Because, Scott, there was a plan—a grand plan."

There was little need for Bauval to say any more. I knew he was right, although it had taken me many years of research on my own to become convinced of such a grand plan. Conventional Egyptology, however, has little time for such suggestions. To the Egyptologists the pyramids—all of them—simply reflected the will of the particular king in whose name each pyramid was supposedly built (as his eternal tomb). Ideas of a preconceived, grand, unified plan are summarily dismissed. The pyramids, the Egyptologists insist, were singular, royal funerary edifices built in splendid isolation on the whim of the ruling king with little or no regard for what had gone before or would come after. In short, the pyramids were not built to satisfy the requirements of any grand, preconceived plan, as a growing number of independent researchers have long argued, but each one is simply the tomb of each individual ancient Egyptian king.

Of course, for Egyptologists to accept the notion that there was a grand, preconceived, transgenerational project that had been set in motion by the ancient Egyptians to build a whole series of giant pyramids (about sixteen of them) would place a serious question mark over the Egyptologists' tomb theory, so it is understandable why most Egyptologists have rejected such ideas out of hand; a "grand, preconceived plan" and the "tombs of kings" are essentially ideas that are regarded as being mutually exclusive. However, as will be demonstrated throughout the course of this book, the evidence in support of such a preconceived, transgenerational grand plan is considerable and should not be so readily dismissed.

Snaking up the plateau, Bauval and I veered off to the right in the direction of the Great Pyramid. From where I was now standing, close to its southeast corner, the light was just right for me to see what I had come here and hoped, on that special day of the year, to observe. It is a feature of the Great Pyramid that was first observed by early European pyramid explorers at the beginning of the eighteenth century and is probably best described by modern Egyptologist J. P. Lepre.

> One very unusual feature of the Great Pyramid is a concavity of the core that makes the monument an eight-sided figure, rather than four-sided like every other Egyptian pyramid. That is to say, that its four sides are hollowed in or indented along their central lines, from base to peak. This concavity divides each of the apparent four sides in half, creating a very special and unusual eight-sided pyramid; and it is executed to such an extraordinary degree of precision as to enter the realm of the uncanny. For, viewed from any ground position or distance, this concavity is quite invisible to the naked eye. The hollowing-in can be noticed only from the air, and only at certain times of the day. This explains why virtually every available photograph of the Great Pyramid does not show the hollowing-in phenomenon, and why the concavity was never discovered until the age of aviation. It was discovered quite by accident in 1940, when a British Air Force pilot, P. Groves, was flying over the pyramid. He happened to notice the concavity and captured it in the now-famous photograph.[1]

Lepre's account of the discovery of this phenomenon is not quite accurate since, during the equinox of March 21, 1934, French Egyptologist André Pochan had photographed the south side of the Great Pyramid, where he observed that the western side (triangle) of the pyramid's southern face was lighter than the opposite eastern triangle. Pochan believed that there was a clear purpose for this phenomenon, regarding it as a marker for the equinoxes. Pochan's discovery was published in a communication to the Institute of Egypt in September 1935. Some five years later the famous aerial photograph of this phenomenon was taken by Groves.

Certainly before 1940 there were very few (if any) aerial photographs of the Great Pyramid that allowed this peculiar feature of the structure to be observed. Nevertheless, contrary to what Lepre has stated in his book, this feature of the Great Pyramid can indeed be observed from the ground under favorable lighting conditions, as Pochan's photos have shown and as I could now observe for myself. There it was—the southern face of the Great Pyramid seemingly split into two halves due to the different shades of light cast from the sun rising due east, sideways onto the ever-so-slightly indented (southern) slope of the pyramid. And though it is often difficult to observe this peculiar phenomenon of the pyramid throughout the year, the slightly inward-leaning concave faces of the pyramid that bring about this astronomical event are physical features that are most certainly measurable, as noted by pioneering Egyptologist Sir William Matthew Flinders Petrie, whom many regard as the father of modern Egyptology. He writes, "I continually observed that the courses of the core had dips of as much as ½° to 1°."[2]

Also contrary to what Lepre writes, there is in fact one other pyramid—the Pyramid of Menkaure (G3) at Giza—that also clearly exhibits this peculiar eight-sided feature. However, of the 138 or so known pyramids in Egypt today, these are the only two pyramids (figure 1.2) that clearly demonstrate these peculiar concave faces, and, suffice it to say, it is a feature of these pyramids that conventional Egyptology struggles to reasonably explain. What could this

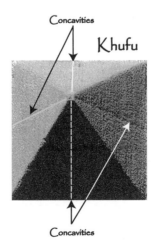

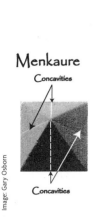

Figure 1.2. The concave slopes of G1 (right) and G3

feature mean, and why do we find it only in the largest and smallest of the main pyramids at Giza? Why not also in the middle pyramid of Khafre (G2) or in the other giant pyramids at Abu Roash, Saqqara, Meidum, or Dahshur?

The precision with which these indented slopes were executed on the four faces of these two pyramids demonstrates that they were clearly intended from the outset in the design of the pyramids, and the considerable additional effort required to construct them implies that they were integral to the pyramid's design right from the outset and were clearly designed to serve some very specific purpose.

Certainly designing the Great Pyramid with these slightly inward-sloping elevations means that it can function as an effective equinoctial marker (as Pochan suggested), essentially marking when day and night are of equal length, when the days will become longer and the nights shorter, and, of course, vice versa on the autumnal equinox. And it stands to reason that for the pyramid to successfully function as an equinoctial "clock," it would be imperative for the builders to ensure that the structure was perfectly aligned to the cardinal directions, otherwise this phenomenon would not appear exactly on the equinox. In this regard it is no surprise to find that the Great Pyramid is one of the most accurately aligned structures in the world, being only three-sixtieths of one degree from being perfectly aligned to the cardinal directions, an alignment error that is smaller than that of the Greenwich Observatory.

But there is a problem with this idea of marking the equinoxes. If this was indeed the intent of the builders, then to do such requires only *one* structure with these concave faces. So why did the builders opt to make their construction issues doubly difficult by building *two* pyramids at Giza with these concave faces when, as stated, one such structure would have sufficed? Or is it perhaps the case that some other underlying rationale is involved here to explain the decision to build *two* eight-sided pyramids? It was the answer to this particular question that would ultimately lead me to a breakthrough in the understanding of these peculiar features built into these two pyramids, and it was an answer that has the potential to change everything we think we know about the builders of these ancient monuments and, indeed, why they built them.

There also are hints from antiquity that the eight-sided nature of these two pyramids at Giza was known then and that there was some significance attached to them. Curiously, if we imagine this eight-sided pyramid flattened onto the ground, it presents to us the form of a Templar Cross, an ancient symbol of which the eminent 32nd-Degree Freemason Frank C. Higgins tells us:

> The characteristic crosses of the Knights Templar, which are faithfully reproduced by the modern Masonic fraternity, are not Calvary crosses, or the type signifying the supreme drama of Christian faith, but four-fold triangles joined at the apexes, the same being identical with a form highly symbolic throughout the ancient East from a period as remote as several thousand years before Christ. They are shown in company with representations of the sun, moon and stars and various zodiacal signs suspended from the necks of the ancient Assyrian and Babylonian monarchs. They are in fact, flattened pyramids and possess the same significance.[3]

It seems then that the Templar Cross (figure 1.3) depicting the eight-sided pyramid suggests that knowledge of the concavities of the Great Pyramid had been observed long ago and also that some significance was known to have been attributed to these curious features. Why else would Higgins tell us "they [Templar Crosses] are in fact, flattened pyramids and possess the same significance"?

But what significance?

It was a question I would revisit time and time again, seeking an answer. What was abundantly clear to me was that the designers and builders must have placed these peculiar features into these two pyramids for a very specific reason for, in so doing, they were going

Figure 1.3. The Templar Cross

out of their way to make the construction of these two pyramids so much more difficult for themselves. Why build a complex eight-sided structure when a four-sided pyramid would have been so much simpler? These were clearly no accidents of design. There *had* to be a reason for them.

As the sun rose ever higher above and around the eastern horizon, casting more light uniformly onto the southern slope of the Great Pyramid, the two different triangular shadows gradually merged into one, removing the split-face effect from its southern elevation and returning the structure to the conventional four-sided pyramid we are familiar with. But I had witnessed this strange phenomenon with my own eyes and was thrilled at having done so. Having read so much about this effect in numerous books and having puzzled over its purpose for so long, this curious effect was now *real* to me and not merely some abstract concept that bland words on a page struggled to properly convey. The phenomenon really did exist, and, as far as I was concerned, these subtle and inexplicable features on the four sides of these two pyramids at Giza presented a clue to something of great import, a clue that I believed might hold the key to uncovering the location of the legendary hidden chamber of Osiris, a secret vault that a number of ancient texts (Egyptian, Greek, and Roman) suggested had been buried in remote antiquity and that legend further tells us holds within it the "wisdom of Osiris."

WHISPERS OF THE CHAMBER

The idea that there is a hidden chamber preserving some form of high wisdom passed down from remote antiquity is as old as Egypt itself, and countless numbers of individuals and groups have sought to discover and prove the existence of such a chamber for almost as long—even into modern times. Understandably, most of the searching for hidden chambers that has taken place—especially in recent times—has focused on the Giza pyramid complex and the area around the Sphinx, much of it driven by the "readings" of the so-called Sleeping Prophet, Edgar Cayce, who in 1932 during one of his readings prophesied, "With the storehouse, or record house (where the records are still to be uncovered), there is a chamber or passage from the right forepaw [of the Sphinx] to this entrance of the record chamber, or record tomb. This may not be entered without an understanding."[4]

Of course, had Cayce's writings been the only source suggesting the existence of a hidden chamber containing ancient records, then the very idea that such might actually be real would seem to exist more in the realm of fantasy than in any actual possibility, and for anyone to embark on a quest to find such a hidden chamber on such a premise would, naturally, be considered something of a romantic, crazy, and somewhat forlorn dream. However, placing Cayce's unproven "prophecies" aside, we can turn to a number of ancient sources that present us with tantalizing hints as to the presence of a hidden vault somewhere at Giza (or close by), and furthermore, some of these ancient sources also hint as to why it was deemed necessary to create such a secret chamber. As author and researcher Joseph Robert Jochmans explains:

> In the Corpus Hermeticum, a body of treatises compiled from older materials toward the beginning of the Christian era, we find in one of these works, the *Virgin of the World,* the following:
>
> "The sacred symbols of the cosmic elements, the secrets of Osiris, were hidden carefully. Hermes (the Greek equivalent to the ancient

Egyptian god, Thoth), before his return to Heaven, invoked a spell on them, and said, O holy books which have been made by my immortal hands, by incorruption's magic spell remain free from decay throughout eternity and incorrupt by time. Become unseeable, unfindable, from everyone whose foot shall tread the plains of this land, until old Heaven shall bring instruments for you, whom the Creator shall call His souls. Thus spake he, and laying the spells on them by means of his works, he shut them safe away in their rooms. And long has been the time since they were hid away."

The Roman Marcellinus, in the 4th century, stated: "There are certain subterranean galleries and passages full of windings beneath the pyramids which, it is said, the adepts in the ancient rites (knowing that the flood was coming, and fearing that the memory of the sacred ceremonies would be obliterated), constructed vaults in various places, mining them out of the ground with great labor. . . ."

In similar fashion, the tenth century Coptic chronicler Al Masudi observed from earlier accounts that in the area of the Sphinx were subterranean doorways to the Giza monuments: "One entered the pyramid through a vaulted underground passage 100 cubits or more long; each pyramid had such a door and entry."

In later centuries, the medieval Arab chronicler Firouzabadi noted that the chambers of the Sphinx were constructed at the same time as the Great Pyramid: "The Pyramid was erected by Esdris (Hermes or Thoth), to preserve there the sciences, to prevent their destruction. And also, the first priests, by observations of the stars, preserved records of medicine, magic and talismans elsewhere." Likewise, Ibn Abd Alhokim, who told the story of the antediluvian king Salhouk's dream of the Flood and his building of the Pyramid to save wisdom, also recounted that Salhouk dug a vault nearby the Pyramid, filling it with all manners of works on mathematics, astronomy and physics: "And they built gates (entrances) of it forty cubits underground, with foundations of massive stones from the Ethiopians, and fastened them together with lead and iron. When

Salhouk was finished, he covered it with colored marble from top to bottom and he appointed a solemn festival, at which were present all the inhabitants of the kingdom."

The Jewish historian Josephus recorded further that Enoch built an underground temple of nine vaults, one beneath the other, placing within tablets of gold. His son, Methuselah, also worked on the project, putting in the brick walls of the vaults according to his father's plan. As Manly P. Hall noted, the Freemasons predict that someday a man will locate this buried vault.[5]

The early Arab chronicles further tell us *why* the ancient Egyptians deemed it necessary to build their monumental pyramids.

There was a king named Surid, the son of Sahaloe, 300 years before the Deluge, who dreamed one night that he saw the earth overturned with its inhabitants, the men cast down on their faces, the stars falling out of the heavens, and striking one against the other, and making horrid and dreadful cries as they fell. He thereupon awoke much troubled. A year after he dreamed again that he saw the fixed stars come down to the earth in the form of white birds, which carried men away, and cast them between two great mountains, which almost joined together and covered them; and then the bright, shining stars became dark and were eclipsed. Next morning he ordered all the princes of the priests, and magicians of all the provinces of Egypt, to meet together; which they did to the number of 130 priests and soothsayers, with whom he went and related to them his dream.

Among others, the priest Aclimon, who was the greatest of all, and resided chiefly in the king's Court, said thus to him:—I myself had a dream about a year ago which frightened me very much, and which I have not revealed to anyone. I dreamed, said the priest, that I was with your Majesty on the top of the mountain of fire, which is in the midst of Emosos, and that I saw the heaven sink down below its ordinary situation, so that it was near the crown of our heads, covering and surrounding us, like a great basin turned upside down; that the stars were intermingled among men in diverse figures; that the people implored your Majesty's succor, and ran to you in multitudes as their refuge; that you lifted up your hands above your head, and endeavored to thrust back the heaven, and keep it from coming down so low; and that I, seeing what your Majesty did, did also the same. While we were in that posture, extremely affrighted, I thought we saw a certain part of heaven opening, and a bright light coming out of it; that afterwards the sun rose out of the same place, and we began to implore his assistance; whereupon he said thus to us: "The heaven will return to its ordinary situation when I shall have performed three hundred courses." I thereupon awaked extremely affrighted.

The priest having thus spoken, the king commanded them to take the height of the stars, and to consider what accident they portended. Whereupon they declared that they promised first the Deluge, and after that fire. Then he commanded pyramids should be built, that they might remove and secure in them what was of most esteem in their treasuries, with the bodies of the kings, and their wealth, and the aromatic roots which served them, and that they should write their wisdom upon them, that the violence of the water might not destroy it.[6]

In a similar vein, world-renowned Egyptologist Mark Lehner, Ph.D., writes:

A Coptic legend tells of King Surid who lived three centuries before the flood. His dreams foretold future chaos and only those who joined the Lord of the Boat would escape. . . . Surid may be a corruption of Suphis, a late form of Khufu, his city, Amsus, is Memphis and the Lord of the Boat is an amalgam of Noah's Ark and the barque of the sun god.

Another popular Arab legend maintained that the Great Pyramid was the tomb of Hermes—the Greek counterpart of the Egyptian Thoth—who, like Surid, built pyramids to hide literature and science from the uninitiated and preserve them through the flood. . . .

Embellishments of the Arab legends abounded, including of the Surid story. The 15th century historian al-Maqrizi reported that the king decorated the walls and the ceilings of his pyramid chambers with representations of the stars and planets and all the sciences, and placed treasures within such. . . . Maqrizi also says that, according to the Copts, Surid was buried in the pyramid surrounded by all his possessions. If Surid is a memory of Khufu, this may not be so far from the truth.[7]

While parts of these Arab legends are presented in the form of a dream, it is important to note that the king (Surid) related this dream to his advisors and, having so done, he then ordered that they "take the height of the stars." Upon doing this it is clear that the astronomer-priests found something unusual and troublesome in the heavens as they advise the king that three hundred years hence the land will be devastated by a great deluge and fire (drought). This activity of the priests in measuring the height of the stars was not a part of the king's dream; the king ordered this to be done *afterward*. And it was only upon hearing this deeply troublesome news of deluge and drought from his astronomer-priests that the king then ordered the construction of the pyramids to safeguard in them that which was of most esteem in the kingdom. Again, the deluge and fire and the subsequent order to construct the pyramids were not part of the king's original dream.

But why should parts of this Arab legend be relayed in the form of the "king's dream"? To people of the ancient world dreams were very motivational; the king certainly took them seriously as it was believed that dreams were in fact "messages from the gods." As such dreams (or messages from the gods) given to the king acted in a sense to confer the "power of the gods" on the king himself. For this reason this story of Surid's dream may have come down to us in this form; the vehicle of relating the story via the "king's dream" demonstrates the power of the king, that the king himself was a god and possessed the power of the gods, that through his dreams he received their "messages." In short, through these "dreams" the king possessed the power of the gods. We are reminded here, of course, of the Bible story of Joseph interpreting the pharaoh's dream, and upon hearing Joseph's interpretation of his dream, the Pharaoh then ordered the construction of large granaries—all on the basis of a dream, a "message from the gods."

In a similar vein, researcher and author Gary Osborn writes:

The Roman historian Ammianus Marcellinus (born circa 330 AD) speculated that the pyramids were vaults containing ancient wisdom.

Then there's the journals of a Moroccan named Ibn Battuta. Between 1325 and 1355 Battuta trekked back-and-forth through the lands of Islam. Apparently he claims to have travelled more than 75,000 miles by foot and on camel. He learned of many things from the wise men and mystics he met while travelling, and wrote everything down in his journal. He especially wrote of a man named Hermes Trismegistus whose wisdom made him equatable with the god Thoth, and whom Battuta learned was also the Hebrew Enoch.

This man, he writes, who "having ascertained from the appearance of the stars that the deluge would take place, built the pyramids to contain books of science and knowledge, and other matters worth preserving from oblivion and ruin."

Then there's Sir John Mandeville. His book "The Travels" (c. 1366) included descriptions of the pyramids, which the author suggests were the "granaries of Joseph":

"And now also I shall speak of another thing that is beyond Babylon, above the flood of the Nile, toward the desert between Africa and Egypt; that is to say, of the garners [granaries] of Joseph, that he let make for to keep the grains for the peril of the dear years. And they be made of stone, full well made of masons' craft; of which two be marvelously great and high, and the other ne be not so great. And every garner hath a gate for to enter within, a little high from the earth; for the land is wasted and fallen since the garners were made. And within they be all full of serpents. And above the garners without be many scriptures of diverse languages. And some men say, that they be sepulchers of great lords, that were sometime, but that is not true, for all the common rumor and speech is of all the people there, both far and near, that they be the garners of Joseph; and so find they in their scriptures, and in their chronicles. On the other part, if they were sepulchers, they should not be void within, ne they should have no gates for to enter within; for ye may well know, that tombs and sepulchers be not made of such greatness, nor of such highness; wherefore it is not to believe, that they be tombs or sepulchers."

George Sandys, (1578–1644) who had entered Oxford in 1589, was the youngest of the seven sons of Edwin Sandys, the former Bishop of London and Archbishop of York. The Sandys lineage has a colorful past—many of them maintaining high-standing positions in both state religion and politics.

Nothing more is known of George Sandys until 1610, when seeking adventure, he left England on a grand tour of the east, spending a year in Turkey, Palestine and Egypt. Sandys was one of the first educated Europeans to enter the Great Pyramid, remarking that, "contrary to popular opinion, the pyramids are the tombs of kings."

It seems that this [issue] was being argued even then and that popular opinion at the time was that the pyramids were NOT tombs.[8]

Of this anticipated deluge, the ancient Egyptians themselves tell us this:

Then Thoth, being the tongue of the Great God declares that, acting for the Lord Tem, he is going to make a Flood. He says: "I am going to blot out everything that I have made. This Earth shall enter into (i.e., be absorbed in) the watery abyss of Nu (or Nunu) by means of a raging flood, and will become even as it was in primeval time. I myself shall remain together with Osiris, but I shall transform myself into a small serpent, which can be neither comprehended nor seen." Budge explains ". . . one day the Nile will rise and cover all Egypt with water, and drown the whole country; then, as in the beginning, there will be nothing to be seen except water."[9]

What all of this alludes to is that there seems to have been an ancient tradition that associates the construction of the earliest pyramids (the giant pyramids) of ancient Egypt as providing some form of protection (a form of "doomsday vault" or "ark") against an anticipated deluge that the ancient Egyptians *believed* would destroy their entire kingdom, a great deluge that they believed to be imminent after they had observed that the path of the stars had changed from their normal course (i.e., that the Earth's axis had been disturbed in some way). In building these giant, immovable "storehouses," the ancient Egyptians could place within them everything that would be needed to help ensure that their kingdom and culture could revive and reconstitute itself after the worst effects of this anticipated deluge had passed.

In summary, anticipating an impending natural disaster that they feared would completely destroy their civilization, the ancient Egyptians set in motion a "national disaster-recovery plan" (Project Osiris?) that saw them, over a few generations, complete a series of pyramids (about sixteen in total) that would essentially serve as arks that they hoped would bring about their cultural revival after the worst effects of the anticipated cataclysm had subsided, a concept that is not too dissimilar to our modern Svalbard Global Seed Vault in the Arctic Circle, which was secured in 2008.

What is important to understand here is that the catalyst event that so motivated the ancient Egyptians to initiate this national disaster-recovery project (i.e., the building of the first pyramids) was quite separate from the anticipated disaster that the king and his astronomer-priests believed was to follow and that the pyramids were built to survive. As stated, the catalyst event that *initiated* the construction of the pyramids (according to these ancient sources) seems to have been a sudden change in the course of the heavens (i.e., a disturbance of the Earth's rotational axis), and the king, in asking his advisors what this change in the heavens would mean, was told that it would (some three hundred years in the future) result in a great deluge and fire (drought). It was only upon hearing of this impending disaster that the king then ordered the immediate construction of the pyramids as places in which to secure those items that were deemed most important to enable the kingdom to flourish again after the worst effects of the anticipated future calamities had passed.

But did the king's astronomer-priests actually observe some abnormal change in the heavens? Was the Earth's rotational axis disturbed in some way, causing the stars to change their course, and was this event followed three hundred years later by a great deluge and drought? Well, *something* seems to have happened, and this will be discussed in chapter 7. The simple point here, however, is that whether the anticipated disaster actually came to pass is actually neither here nor there; the key point is that the ancient Egyptians as a result of their observations of the heavens, *believed* a disaster was imminent and were motivated enough by this belief to put in place measures to try to protect themselves against its catastrophic effects, to try to put in place the means through which their kingdom could recover after its coming demise.

In short, if the ancient accounts are correct, then it seems that the ancient Egyptians *believed* their civilization was in great peril from deluge and drought and sought to take what they believed was the best possible course of action in an attempt to try to at least secure the recovery of their kingdom after the anticipated disaster; that is, they initiated their Project Osiris and built their pyramid arks as part of a precautionary national disaster-recovery plan.

THE SEEN AND THE UNSEEN

Of course, in planning and building their pyramid arks or "recovery vaults" it stands to reason that whatever was created would need to be constructed to be as strong as possible to withstand the full force of nature and built as large as possible to ensure maximum visibility from great distances in order that they could be found as quickly as possible (sooner rather than later). There would be little point in placing such arks underground or within a natural mountain, because such natural features simply would not stand out in the natural environment and would most likely result in the arks *never* being found. The arks needed to be *artificial mountains* in order to be obvious, to stand out in the natural environment. And as stated previously, they also needed to be built as strong and as secure as possible to withstand the full force of nature (a great deluge and drought), requiring innovative engineering in the use of truly colossal stone blocks. The combined storage capacity of the arks' internal chambers would require sufficient volume to store as much "recovery goods" as possible from which to reseed the kingdom.

But while the early, giant pyramid arks (being so highly visible) would have been easily seen and, therefore, found relatively quickly (thus facilitating the quick recovery of essential items such as tools, seeds, storage and distribution vessels, etc.), this would have satisfied only one requirement of the recovery plan—providing quick access to those items that were absolutely essential for survival; that is, the production of a sustainable food supply. But what of other items such as ancient records and other "secondary treasures" that, while important and precious to the civilization in their own right, were not actually regarded as vital for immediate survival? After all, when there is no food such "precious" items are of little use or value. A trinket of gold cannot be eaten.

It would have made little sense to store such secondary precious items in the highly visible pyramid arks because, were this to have been done, then it would have been known to the builders (i.e., the population at large) that such secondary treasures had been placed within the structures along with the primary recovery items and would have made the pyramid arks targets for thieves the moment they were sealed, thereby compromising the viability of the essential, primary recovery items that had been placed within. However, were it known to the builders that the pyramids would be storing *only* the essential recovery items (e.g., seeds, storage and distribution vessels, tools, etc.), then the populace would realize that the reward for breaching the colossal pyramid arks would hardly be commensurate with the great effort involved. No one would bother raiding the pyramid arks for such items, because it would be easier by far to simply nip down to the local market for seeds, tools, and such.

A far better and more logical solution for the safe and secure storage of nonvital but otherwise precious cultural items would be to store these secondary items in another type of recovery vault that was not a highly visible pyramid ark but rather a hidden chamber deep underground, a vault that would have no directly visible marker indicating its location, a secret chamber that would become engulfed and lost to the Egyptian sands. In short, it would make more sense to store such secondary valuable items within a chamber that was hidden and undiscoverable—just as some of the ancient texts describe.

FOUND BY THREE

Of course, simple logic dictates that there would have to be *some* means created by the designers that would assist in the relocation of such a hidden chamber. It would not make sense for the builders to place their nonvital but otherwise precious cultural items into a vault deep underground, cover it completely with rock and sand, and merely *hope* that someday it may be recovered by accident or good fortune. It stands to reason that the designers would not have relinquished the rediscovery of their hidden vault containing items of great cultural value merely to chance and would have gone out of their way to create and include some means by which the precise whereabouts of the hidden underground vault could be determined and the precious cultural items contained therein recovered. In this regard, Jochmans further writes:

> In another Egyptian text, known today as the Westcar Papyrus, which bears evidence of dating to the Fourth Dynasty, is the story of an enigmatic sage named Djeda who could not only perform miraculous feats of magic, but who also possessed certain information concerning what he called the secret chambers of the books of Thoth. In the narrative, Djeda told Pharaoh Khufu the location of specific keys that will one day open the hidden place, which he described as follows:
>
> In the city of Ani (Heliopolis) is a temple called the House of Sapti, referring to Septi, the fifth Pharaoh of the First Dynasty, who reigned about 3000 B.C. Within the temple is a special library room where the scrolls of inventory are kept. The walls of this room are made of sandstone blocks, and either within or behind one of these blocks is a secret niche containing a small box made of flint or whetstone. It is within this box that the ipwt-seals or keys that will open the secret chambers of Thoth, the Hall of Records, may still be hidden.
>
> When Khufu asked Djeda to bring these keys to him, the sage replied he did not have the power to do so, but prophesied that he who some day would find the keys would be one of three sons born to Rad-dedet, the wife of the chief priest of Ra in Heliopolis, Lord of Sakhbu (the second Lower Egyptian nome or district in the Nile Delta), and that the three would be born on the 15th day of the month of Tybi (our October–November).
>
> Now it is generally interpreted that the three mentioned were the first three Pharaohs of the succeeding Fifth Dynasty. But because much of Egyptian literature is multi-leveled in its symbolism, there is reason to believe that a more hidden meaning may have been intended, that the three enigmatic brothers may also be those yet

future individuals who will one day find and open the Hall of Records.[10]

When I first read this tale or myth of Djeda and the other accounts of hidden chambers in or around Giza, it immediately struck me that the "three enigmatic brothers" in question that would one day find the hidden chamber may not actually be pharaohs per se, or even people, but rather the three giant pyramids (attributed to three pharaohs) at Giza. This is to say that the three giant pyramids at Giza may allegorically represent the three brothers or three kings. In this regard we are further reminded of the words of the nineteenth-century antiquarian Gerald Massey, who wrote, "For the 'Three Kings' is still a name of the three stars of Orion's Belt."[11]

If the three grand pyramids at Giza are a symbolic representation of Orion's Belt (as proposed by Robert Bauval and Adrian Gilbert in their book *The Orion Mystery*), then, by extension, these structures can surely also be considered as the "Three Kings." It is noteworthy here to point out that, in the Northern Hemisphere, Orion's Belt is best observed in the autumn months (from around October to November), when it is more easily seen. Could it be that this most prominent appearance of Orion in October and November is an allegory of Djeda's "the three would be born on the 15th day of the month of Tybi [our October–November]." And if these Three Kings (i.e., three pyramids of Giza) might have held the secret wisdom as to the whereabouts of a hidden ark or vault, then it is not unreasonable that they might also have been considered as "Three Wise Men." In this regard, Lynn Picknett and Clive Prince write:

> We were also struck by this statement in Cocteau's journal, about a night-time visit to the pyramids of Giza:
> "In the sky lies the unharnessed Wain, shafts pointing upwards. Strange stopping place! The Three Wise Men have struck their tents of stone, stretched from base to point, one side in the shadow and

the other three smoothed by the moon. They sleep while their dog lies awake. Their watch dog is the Sphinx." [*Cocteau Maalesh: A Theatrical Tour in the Middle East.* Paris: Gallimard, 1949, 37.]

"Three Wise Men" is the French term for the three stars we know as Orion's Belt. There was a media sensation when Robert Bauval and Adrian Gilbert's *The Orion Mystery* was published in 1994, arguing that the three pyramids of Giza were built specifically to represent Orion's Belt. Yet here we have Cocteau, in 1949, apparently taking the connection for granted![12]

So Djeda's story may indeed be allegorical in nature and a more hidden meaning intended, as Jochmans believes. And it may also be that the means by which to locate the hidden chamber is presented to us in plain sight, right under our very noses, by three of the largest man-made monuments on Earth—the Three Brothers, Three Kings, or Three Wise Men.

In building their great pyramid arks to contain vital recovery items, the designers may *also* have used these very same structures, the three giant Giza pyramids, in a quite ingenious way to encode the precise location of the legendary hidden chamber of Osiris, the ancient Egyptian god who is personified by the constellation of Orion, known across the ages as the Three Kings and the Three Wise Men. And the "keys" to determine the whereabouts of the hidden vault?

The *concavities* of the Giza pyramids!

It is often said that seeing is believing. Well, for me, seeing with my own eyes on that chilly spring equinox dawn the shaded triangles formed by the concavities of the Great Pyramid sent a ripple of excitement and anticipation running down my spine; yes, they were a trick of the light, but nonetheless, they really did exist. No doubt. And, as noted already, they obviously existed for a reason whose importance seems to have far outweighed the considerable additional construction burden their inclusion would have posed the builders. There was a *reason* for them; they were the *keys*.

For the first time since formulating my theory on the concavities of the Giza pyramids I was beginning to feel that I had reason to believe that the understanding and rationale I had come to regarding these odd features were more than simply a leap of faith, that quite possibly I was on the right track and that my journey here to Egypt to search for (and hopefully discover) the legendary hidden chamber of Osiris might bring more success than I had ever dared to imagine. I was, after all, pursuing a mere theory and was still a very long way from proving its veracity. But the concavities *were* real, and observing their effect with my own eyes offered me hope, raised my expectation of success, even if only a little. The presence of these enigmatic features in G1 and G3 was perhaps to provide an ever-so-subtle hint, but their significance, if I was right, would be truly monumental.

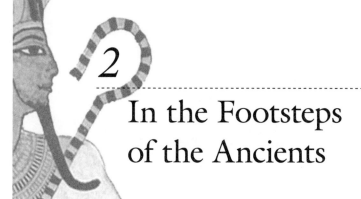

2

In the Footsteps
of the Ancients

Know ye that in the pyramid I builded are the KEYS that shall show ye the WAY into life; aye, draw ye a line from the great image, I builded, to the apex of the pyramid, built as a gateway. Draw ye another opposite in the same angle and direction, dig ye and find that which I have hidden. There shall ye find the underground entrance, to the secrets hidden before ye were men.

DOREAL, *THE EMERALD TABLETS*
OF *THOTH-THE-ATLANTEAN*

As noon approached it was much hotter, approaching 35°C. My taxi driver had finally dropped me off on the sand-blown asphalt road near to the now disused and somewhat dilapidated amphitheater just to the west of G2, the pyramid attributed to Khafre. And, I have to say, it was with some considerable anxiety and trepidation that I watched him turn and drive away, vanishing into the horizon in a haze of shimmering heat, leaving me alone in an area of the plateau that very few ever

31

visited these days. I could have been dropped off farther along the desert road, nearer to my destination, but I wanted the opportunity to capture the giant pyramids from a perspective that few ever enjoyed. Without doubt, it was going to be a long, arduous, and extremely uncomfortable trek back. I just hoped at that point that it would all be worth the effort.

Having rubbed some more sunblock onto my arms and neck, I took a few tentative paces in the direction of the derelict amphitheater. Throughout the 1990s this open-air theater that seated around four thousand people had been the centerpiece of a grand light and sound show that featured Verdi's *Aida,* an opera based on a tale first penned in 1869 by pioneering French Egyptologist Auguste Mariette. The opera portrayed the tragic story of a love triangle between an Ethiopian princess/slave girl (Aida), an Egyptian military commander, and the pharaoh's daughter. With the giant pyramids of Giza bringing such an appropriate and imposing backdrop, there could be no greater or more fitting setting on Earth for such a production.

But now, standing here under a scorching sun on a dusty and deserted road with only the giant, brooding pyramids for company, the distant echoes of such pomp and splendor seemed light-years away, and the once vibrant amphitheater that played host to those annual operatic triumphs had now decayed into silent ruin, the encroaching desert sands slowly but ever so steadily burying what little remained, just as in Verdi's opera, in which the slave girl Aida, having been lowered into a stone vault with her lover, was buried alive, her life finally extinguished by rising, suffocating sands—a most befitting allegory to the scene that lay before me now.

But time was of the essence. There was a lot to be done, and wandering around the derelict amphitheater was serving only as a distraction. As I turned back toward the road a car appeared out of the haze, flashing by in a blur, followed soon after by a busload of waving, cheering tourists, obviously heading to the viewpoint about a half mile farther down the winding, desert road. They must have wondered what on Earth someone was doing wandering around such a remote part of the plateau in such incredible heat, heading southwest, away from the pyramids, toward the edge of the desert.

I took out a map, found a flat rock, and spread it open, then pored over it for a minute or so, checking my route. I had already marked the location of the amphitheater, my starting point, with a red marker. From here I would have to walk about two miles along the desert road to my next reference point far to the southwest of the pyramid field, and from there just over 1,600 feet due west. Unfortunately my budget could not stretch to the luxury of employing GPS to find this remote and obscure desert location, so I would simply have to find it the good old-fashioned way, using map, compass, pedometer, and fishing line. In my bag I had a reel of fishing line premeasured at 1,606 feet in length—the precise distance I needed to travel due west to my "X" location, my destination and journey's end. The pedometer had been precalibrated to my walking pace, which was fine on a straight and level road, but farther on, in the undulating and rough terrain at the edge of the desert, it would not be nearly so accurate, hence the precisely measured length of fishing line.

Having quenched my thirst, I set off once more, following the desert road in a southwesterly direction, edging gradually deeper into the desert. Skirting past the gap between the pyramids of Khafre (G2) and Menkaure (G3), I could see, far in the distance, a slow-moving camel train followed in quick succession by three or four riders on horseback, galloping at pace across the billowing desert sands. Even though they were far in the distance, it was good to see them; it didn't seem so lonely out here. Occasionally a helicopter would swoop overhead, seemingly from out of nowhere, circling the pyramids before heading back to the helipad to the northwest of Khafre's Pyramid.

What was not so welcome were the occasional Antiquities Guards, patrolling the area on camel and armed to the teeth with semiautomatic firearms. I had seen a couple of them patrolling the area south of Menkaure's Pyramid just before being dropped off from my taxi. They weren't guys to take lightly, and I hoped that I wouldn't come across any on my journey. I could just imagine the scenario:

"What are you doing out here? Where are you going?"

I would smile politely and say, "Oh, I'm just on my way to search for the legendary chamber of Osiris." Or something to that effect.

Either way, I didn't imagine such a scenario would end well. The guard would most likely think that I was a few sandwiches short of a full hamper and should be turned around for my own safety or, alternatively, would begin asking for all manner of official documents such as search permits from the Supreme Council of Antiquities, university affiliation papers, and the like—of which I had absolutely none. And without such official documentation, no one is permitted to search for anything in Egypt, and consequently I would most likely be unceremoniously marched out of the area and probably slapped with a permanent ban. So, for sure, it was important that I should stay alert and try as best as I possibly could to minimize the possibility of any such encounters with officialdom.

As I continued along the desert road toward my destination, I turned back every so often to take a well-deserved view of the great triangular structures that were slowly but ever so surely shrinking away in the distance behind me. It was at that moment that I saw just how the ancient architects of these remarkable monuments had presented to us as big a clue as they possibly could in order to indicate to us the means of discovering the precise whereabouts of the legendary chamber of Osiris. There it was, in front of me, as clear as day and in plain sight—the simple *triangle*. Standing there on that quiet desert road, taking in that grand vista, it all seemed so mundanely obvious—and so very simple. The Three Brothers pointing the way.

But it hadn't always been so. My instinct told me that the concavities of G1 and G3 held the key (the keys of Thoth) to this puzzle, but still I was unable to find the lock. The concavities of G1 and G3 effectively divided the triangular faces of these two pyramids into two smaller triangles, so it seemed to me that the solution lay somewhere in the use of the simple triangle. This shape is ubiquitous at Giza and, as explained in chapter 1, is *especially* highlighted to us in the Great Pyramid's concave sides during the equinoxes, when the larger triangle of the pyramid face is bisected by shades of light into two smaller triangles. Why demonstrate the triangle being bisected? Had this been done to somehow demonstrate some universal truth, to present a clue of some kind?

I knew that before modern satellite technology, triangulation was the means used by land surveyors to determine an unknown point from the angles of two known points. Could the ancient architects have perhaps built some form of triangulation into the Giza pyramids that could act in some way to allow the pyramids to "point" to a secret location? If so, then how might this have been done?

Long before embarking upon my Giza adventure I had spent many months on my home computer drawing all manner of lines from all manner of significant points on a survey drawing of Giza. It eventually became apparent to me that such an exercise was entirely futile. There were simply too many possibilities pointing to too many different potential locations. If the pyramids had been designed in some way to triangulate to a particular unknown point, then it stood to reason that the rationale employed by the designers would ensure that any such triangulation technique could result in only *one* possible unique location being identified. But how could the three pyramids be used collectively to indicate just *one* unique geographical location? Once again I was stumped.

But it often seems to be the case that just when you think your mind has hit a stone wall, that is exactly the tonic it needs, for in hitting that wall it completely cleared my mind of the cluttered debris of redundant ideas and dead ends that had been rattling around for months, allowing me to start again from scratch. However, one thought remained very firmly fixed in my mind: the words of Djeda—"found by three"; these words were never far from my thoughts. "Found by three." The three Giza pyramids seemed the *obvious* "three," but could there be something else, some other fairly obvious "three" that related to triangles that I was not seeing?

THE PENNY DROPS

Up until that moment I had never been a great believer in serendipity, but as I grappled with this seemingly insoluble problem of finding a means by which all three Giza pyramids could collectively be used in a unique manner to somehow indicate a single geographical location, my young son asked me a completely innocuous and random question about triangles for a school math project on which he was working. He wanted to know how to find the center of a triangle. The question was simple enough, and at first there was no spark, no blinding light, no great epiphany. That would happen some minutes after his simple question had time enough to percolate through the filters of my mental reasoning.

I began by explaining to my son that, unlike a circle or a square, a triangle can actually have many *different* "centers." Today we know of 5,389 different ways to plot unique points (centers) within any particular triangle, but in the ancient world only the three simplest triangle centers were known.

Eureka!

My moment of epiphany had arrived.

There it was; in the ancient world only the *three* simplest triangle centers were known! Finally, the light was switched on.

THE TRIPLE CENTROID

The idea was simple enough. Each of the three main pyramids at Giza might represent one of the three triangle centers that were known in the ancient world—three triangle centers that today we know as *incenter, barycenter,* and *circumcenter* (figures 2.1, 2.2, and 2.3).

1. The Incenter

This point requires a circle to be inscribed within the triangle whereby the perimeter of the circle touches all three sides of the triangle. The center of the inscribed circle is then plotted, and this point becomes the triangle's incenter centroid.

Figure 2.1. The incenter centroid

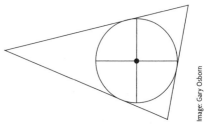

2. The Barycenter

This point requires a line to be drawn from each of the triangle's vertices to the midpoint of the opposite parallel. The intersection where the lines meet is plotted, and this point becomes the triangle's barycenter centroid.

Figure 2.2. The barycenter centroid

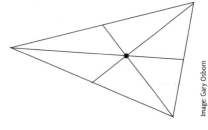

3. The Circumcenter

This point requires a circle to be circumscribed around the triangle in such a way that its perimeter touches all three vertices of the triangle. The center of the circumscribed circle is then plotted, and this point becomes the triangle's circumcenter centroid.

Figure 2.3. The circumcenter centroid

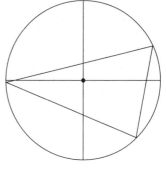

As stated earlier, each and every triangle can contain *all* of these different "centers" at the same time. But depending on the particular shape and orientation of the triangle, the different centers will fall at different relative positions within the triangle (sometimes even *outside* the triangle). In this regard we can consider the three centers of the three pyramids as each belonging to one of the three most ancient triangle centers, and together they could be used to reverse-engineer the unique triangle that contained these three centers; that is, we could use this understanding of the three triangle centers known in the ancient world and determine the unique triangle that matched the particular configuration of the three pyramid centers.

Reverse-engineering this unique triangle was not as easy a task as I had at first imagined, and it involved countless hours in front of a computer screen testing different-shaped triangles, trying to find a unique triangle whose three inherent centers (incenter, circumcenter, and barycenter) matched the relative disposition of the three pyramid centers.

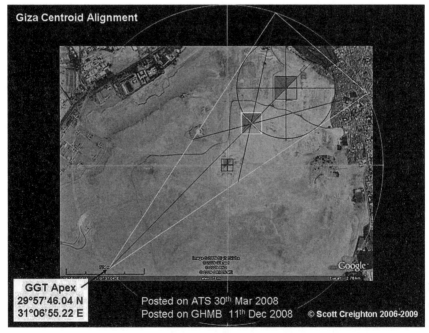

Figure 2.4. The Giza triple centroid triangle

Finally, after many nights falling asleep at my computer desk, I eventually found a triangle (figure 2.4) whose three latent triangle centers (incenter, circumcenter, and barycenter) matched the relative disposition of the three centers of the Giza pyramids.

What is also interesting about this triple-centroid construction is that the cardinally aligned "cross" of the incenter and circumcenter triangles naturally aligns with the lines of the concavities of G1 and G3 and seems to offer an explanation as to why G2 was entirely devoid of these concavities because, being the barycenter of the reverse-engineered Giza triangle, there would be no circle and therefore no cardinally aligned cross to indicate the circle's center. As such, it rather seemed to me, at that point, that the architect of these pyramids had perhaps placed the concavities into G1 and G3 so as to present a subtle hint (the cardinally aligned cross of the concavities alluding to the center of a circle) toward their latent triangle centers in order that these might be used later by someone to reconstruct or reverse-engineer this unique, grand triangle over a plan of the Giza pyramids. And if we consider the two lines that converge at the apex location, we find that both these lines are oriented generally northeast and southwest and have the same angle (figure 2.5)—just as the Emerald Tablets

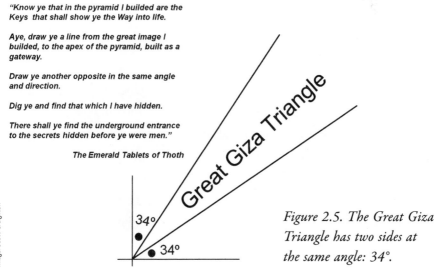

"Know ye that in the pyramid I builded are the Keys that shall show ye the Way into life.

Aye, draw ye a line from the great image I builded, to the apex of the pyramid, built as a gateway.

Draw ye another opposite in the same angle and direction.

Dig ye and find that which I have hidden.

There shall ye find the underground entrance to the secrets hidden before ye were men."

The Emerald Tablets of Thoth

Great Giza Triangle

34°
34°

Figure 2.5. The Great Giza Triangle has two sides at the same angle: 34°.

Image: Scott Creighton

of Thoth indicate to us. These "tablets," which form part of the *Corpus Hermetica,* comprise ancient wisdom texts believed to have been written by the ancient Egyptian god, Thoth the Atlantean, before the Flood.

So here we have two lines drawn toward the same direction of the Giza plateau and at the same angle—but to what end? What exactly would be the point of such a hidden, grand triangle? Well, not to place too fine a point on it, but the point is the triangle's *apex*—its endpoint! This unique triangle actually acts like an arrowhead or pointer that targets a very specific location to the southwest of the Giza plateau on the edge of the desert—the very place I was now headed.

As the Emerald Tablets foretold, "Dig ye and find that which I have hidden. There shall ye find the underground entrance to the secrets hidden before ye were men."[1]

Having identified the apex location of the grand triangle on a map of Giza—an apparently inconsequential area to the southwest of the Giza pyramid field—I knew at once that I simply had to get myself to that location. I knew not, of course, what I would find if and when I ever got there, but it seemed to me, based on the legends of the secret chamber, that it would be "found by three." And the unique nature of the Great Giza Triangle, which itself was "found by three" (i.e., the three pyramid centers corresponding to the three triangle centroids), would be as good a place as any to begin such a search.

But my trip to this remote location in the Egyptian desert would also become something of a pilgrimage, a journey to pay homage to the remarkable builders of these truly awe-inspiring structures. To that end I had taken with me a small pyramid made of Scottish granite—small enough to sit in the palm of my hand. At the apex location I would place my small granite "gift to Osiris" and, in homage, would speak a few words from the "Hymn to Osiris." This hymn contains the most complete account of the Osiris myth ever recorded by the ancient Egyptians, recounting his death at the hands of his treacherous brother Seth and his resurrection and vindication as the true ruler. In reciting these immortal words I felt as though I would be following in the steps of the ancient

Egyptians who venerated this god of rebirth and regeneration; I would also be acknowledging and honoring the tremendous achievement of this ancient people who, by their blood, sweat, and tears, ensured their own (and our) future. And by placing my small pyramid offering at the precise spot the geometry of these great monuments "point" us to, it may also serve as a message to someone who, perhaps ten thousand years from now when our civilization has perhaps been decimated and lost, might understand the same geometry, seek out this very spot, and find this small pyramid that would tell them something of our own civilization.

THE MYTH OF OSIRIS

I'd been traveling along the desert road for about a half hour and had now almost reached the vista point. About six or seven buses were bunched together in a makeshift bus park while dozens of tourists milled around taking snapshots of the pyramids, which thrust out of the desert sands about a mile in the distance. As I turned the sharp bend into the bus park's entrance, from the corner of my eye I caught a glimpse of an Antiquities Guard near the boundary wall at the far side, mounted on a camel, having his photograph taken with some tourists and more than happy to relieve them of some *baksheesh* for his trouble. Or perhaps it was the somewhat unsettling sight of his Glock handgun that compelled the tourists to part with their cash.

This was awkward and precisely the kind of situation I had hoped to avoid. I didn't want to continue on my journey with the guard so near and so able to observe my movements. Not that I was doing or even about to do anything illegal, but it would have looked somewhat peculiar, a lone figure heading out onto the desert road on foot, and would surely have piqued the guard's curiosity and no doubt his attention, which I could well have done without.

Thus, for the next half hour or so I had to stay put and content myself with some sandwiches and my bottle of water—killing time. It was also a convenient opportunity to join the frenzy of pyramid shooting. While this particular aspect of the pyramids—spread out north to south—was truly magnificent, it was not nearly as spectacular a view as the iconic, jaw-dropping, east-west panoramas to be seen from the vantage points to the south of the Giza pyramid field. From the location here the pyramids seemed somehow disjointed, like pieces of a gigantic geometric puzzle that had become scattered and disconnected and that needed to be picked up and reassembled (figure 2.6).

After having taken the third "pyramid-in-my-hand" photo for some grateful American tourists, I overheard the crackling of the guard's radio. He took the radio from his belt and spoke into it briefly before signaling with a brush of his hand, "No more photos." Before long, and with a considerable sense of relief, I watched as he exited from the bus park on his camel, heading out across the desert sand in a southeasterly direction—opposite to where I was headed. I didn't waste any more time. I quickly packed my things and, with one final check that the guard was fully out of sight, made my way once more onto the dusty road.

A few hundred yards later the road took a sharp turn, heading almost exactly due south. In the distance I could see the rise of a small hill, beyond which was my goal. The feeling of excitement and exhilaration was building within me with each passing step. As I looked to the pyramids in the distance behind me, something rather remarkable was occurring—as I reached the point where I was almost perfectly in

Figure 2.6. The Giza pyramids (looking east). Photo by Scott Creighton.

line with the diagonal of the three pyramids, the wide gaps between them had completely vanished, giving the illusion that the three individual structures had morphed into one giant, unified body. In this I was reminded of Plutarch's tale of Osiris and Isis whereby Osiris (the ancient Egyptian god of rebirth and regeneration), having had his body cut into sixteen pieces (some versions of the tale say fourteen pieces) by his evil brother Seth, who then scattered them all across the land of Egypt, was made whole again after his wife (and sister) Isis found all the body parts (with the exception of one) and pieced them together again.

I began to wonder if there was in fact a kernel of truth in this ancient myth, whether it could be possible that this story was actually an allegorical tale pointing us toward a fundamental truth that the body of Osiris that had been cut into sixteen pieces and scattered across the land was not meant to be understood in terms of a human body but was perhaps a metaphorical reference to the early, giant pyramids acting as the body of Osiris, much in the same way that a Christian church today represents the allegorical "body of Christ." And further still, could it be that the one piece of the "body" we are told from the myth that Isis could *not* find may be an allegorical reference to a *hidden* part, a subtle clue to a hidden vault somewhere deep underground, awaiting discovery—the legendary hidden chamber of Osiris?

This may not be as radical a thought as it may at first seem. The idea that the scattered "body of pyramids" (i.e., the first sixteen or so pyramids built by the ancient Egyptians at Abu Roash, Saqqara, Meidum, Dahshur, and Giza) may represent (or may have come in later times to represent) the allegorical body of Osiris finds some support in our earliest religious texts, the ancient Egyptian Pyramid Texts, in which it is written, "This pyramid . . . is Osiris . . . this construction . . . is Osiris."[2]

This notion is given further support in Frank Cole Babbit's translation of Plutarch's *Isis and Osiris,* in which we read, "The traditional result of Osiris's dismemberment is that there are many so-called tombs of Osiris in Egypt; for Isis held a funeral for each part when she had found it . . . all of them called the tomb of Osiris."[3]

While it may have been believed by some later historians such as Plutarch and Herodotus that these early pyramids (along with the hundred or so much later pyramids) had been conceived and built as tombs, there is considerable evidence—presented in the next chapter that raises some serious questions about that assertion. What is absolutely certain, and for which there can be absolutely no doubt, is that clearly *intrusive* burials have been recovered from a number of the earliest pyramids. And, by the same token, what is clear also is that not a single *intact* burial of an ancient Egyptian king has ever been recovered from any of these first pyramids (or indeed from *any* pyramid in any age). Indeed, the *only* fully intact burial of an ancient Egyptian king ever found was that of Tutankhamun, who was buried in a deep, underground tomb (not in a pyramid) in the Valley of the Kings.

The concept of pyramids as arks or recovery vaults for the kingdom (containing all manner of seeds, tools, pottery, etc.) could not be better symbolized than by the ancient Egyptian god Osiris, their god of agriculture and of rebirth. The pyramids contained, after all, the means by which the kingdom hoped to recover should the worst effects of "Thoth's Flood" come to pass. These "dismembered body parts" (i.e., the individual pyramids scattered along the length of the Nile) represented the agency through which the recovery or rebirth of the kingdom could occur.

In essence these first scattered pyramids along the Nile Valley *were* Osiris (i.e., his body cut into sixteen parts), just as the ancient Egyptian Pyramid Texts and Plutarch's *Myth of Osiris* inform us. As such it should be of little surprise then to find that when plotting the individual locations of the first, giant pyramids onto a map of Egypt, what we find is a crude "matchstick" outline drawing of the classic Osiris figurine (see figures 2.7a–e on pages 45–47), complete with the royal regalia of the distinctive three-pronged Atef Crown of Osiris and symbols of power, the crook and flail.

These images demonstrate the locations of the pyramids listed on page 45 with the name of the king Egyptologists believe constructed each pyramid (its location in parentheses), and which were constructed on the high plateaus along the lush green Nile Valley (Osiris is often painted with a green body depicting vegetation and rebirth) and are believed by Egyptologists to have been completed in the following order of construction.

1. Djoser (Saqqara)
2. Sekhemkhet (Saqqara, unfinished)
3. Khaba (Zawiyet al-Aryan, unfinished)
4. Sneferu (Meidum, farthest south)
5. Sneferu (Dahshur, the Bent Pyramid)
6. Sneferu (Dahshur, the Red Pyramid)
7. Khufu (Giza, with four satellite pyramids)
8. Djedefre (Abu Roash, farthest north)
9. Khafre (Giza, with one satellite pyramid)
10. Nebka (Zawiyet al-Aryan, unfinished)
11. Menkaure (Giza, with three satellite pyramids)

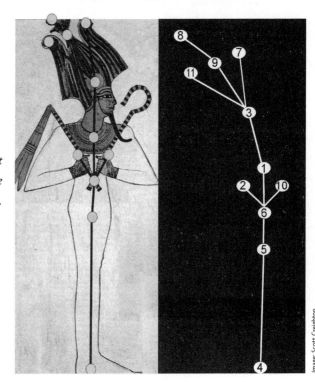

Figure 2.7a. The first pyramids outline the god Osiris.

Image: Scott Creighton

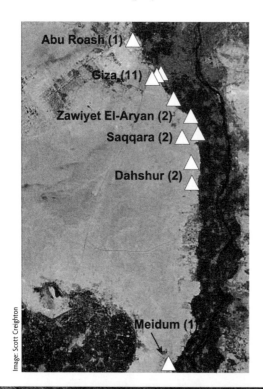

Image: Scott Creighton

Figure 2.7b. Locations of the first 19 pyramids built by the ancient Egyptians along the Nile Valley (inludes 3 unfinished pyramids).

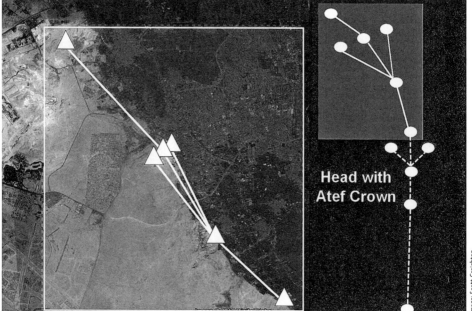

Image: Scott Creighton

Figure 2.7c. The most northern pyramids correlate with the Atef Crown of Osiris.

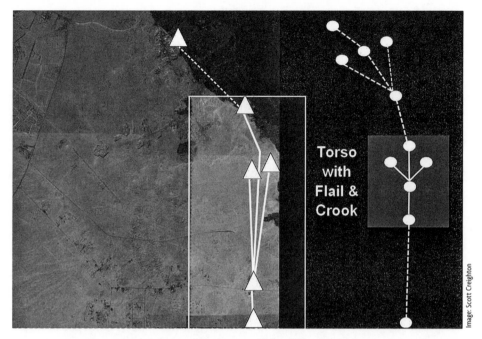

*Figure 2.7d. The middle pyramids correlate with the torso
and the flail and crook of Osiris.*

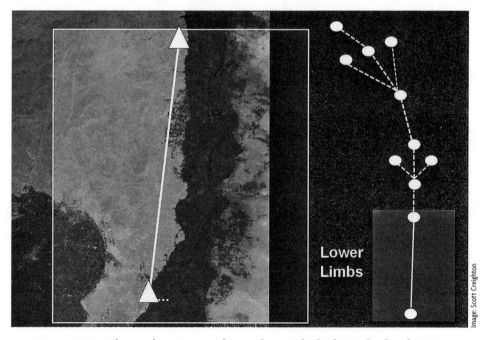

Figure 2.7e. The southern pyramids correlate with the lower limbs of Osiris.

Thus in Dynasties Three and Four we have a grand total of nineteen pyramids, three of which were never finished, giving a total of sixteen completed pyramids. Which brings us back to this possibility: Could the sixteen dismembered parts of the body of Osiris related to us in Plutarch's *Myth of Osiris* actually have been an allegorical reference to the first sixteen pyramids that were completed by the ancient Egyptians? And, as suggested earlier in this chapter, could there perhaps be a secret seventeenth part of this body of Osiris yet to be discovered, the part that Isis could not find?

With each pyramid within the body of Osiris serving as an ark (securing seed such as wheat and barley and other vital recovery items), it is unsurprising to find that in later dynasties during the Festival of Khoiak small effigies of Osiris known as corn mummies would be created and packed full with grain and buried in the ground under a mound of earth or a large rock—the body of Osiris packed full with grain just like the pyramid body of Osiris had once been. (This idea will be discussed in greater detail in chapter 9.)

As I gazed from the desert road along the diagonal of the pyramids, their appearance from this spot as a single giant body (of Osiris) made complete sense to me, and it also made sense of the religious festivals that had arisen in later dynasties in the name of this ancient Egyptian god. Looking back toward these magnificent structures that had now seemingly morphed into a single, giant body, it almost seemed as though my hunch that these individual pyramids collectively represented the (dismembered) body of Osiris was being vindicated. It rather seemed to me that the conventional idea that these structures had been conceived and built as individual royal tombs by a succession of ancient Egyptian kings without any master plan having ever been involved was fundamentally wrong, an outdated premise that had served only to misdirect and misinform for almost two hundred years.

And now, as I turned my back on the pyramids to resume my hitherto trouble-free journey of discovery, it was then that fate decided it would step in with a sharp wake-up call, bringing about a turn of events that would see matters take a sudden and distinct turn for the worse.

3

A Wrong Turn

Guessing at what shall happily be hid,
As the real purpose of a pyramid.

LORD GEORGE GORDON BYRON,
DON JUAN, CANTO THE EIGHTH, 1823

What was the real purpose of the early, giant pyramids? What, if anything, did they contain? These two questions have been offered an answer by Egyptologists who, for the best part of two hundred years, have regarded these structures as the tombs of ancient Egyptian kings and queens and as the instruments of rebirth that would facilitate the transfiguration of the king's soul into an *akh* (an effective being of light), whereupon it could pass unharmed through the Duat (the underworld) and hopefully onward into an undisturbed, everlasting afterlife among the gods of the "Imperishable Ones"; that is, the stars of the northern skies.

The idea that these structures were conceived and built as tombs is all-pervasive to our modern mind-set, so much so that many have come to accept the pyramid tomb theory as being not so much a theory but an actual fact. This is, after all, what many of us were taught in school.

49

So why then should it be deemed necessary to even think about questioning what many regard as fact?

The first thing to say is that the evidence to support the pyramid tomb theory is actually only circumstantial; this theory is entirely devoid of any direct primary evidence. Neither are there any ancient Egyptian texts that categorically state why the ancient Egyptians conceived and built their pyramids. Indeed, there are some ancient texts that actually state that the pyramids were *not* used as tombs. For example, in the book *Sphinx: History of a Monument,* Christiane Zivie-Coche writes, "Describing the Great Pyramids and the hatred their builders supposedly attracted to themselves, Diodorus follows the tradition of Herodotus; he adds, however, that the pharaohs were never buried in them, but rather that the rulers commanded that their bodies be placed in a secure place that was kept secret."[1]

However, even in the absence of any direct evidence, Egyptologists have managed to build up a considerable case for the pyramid tomb theory based solely on the circumstantial evidence they have uncovered (much of that evidence from later times and back-projected onto the much earlier culture). But just how strong is their case? What, if anything, is there that might cast doubt on the Egyptologists' interpretation of the evidence that brought them to conclude that all pyramids in ancient Egypt were conceived and built as tombs? For it stands to reason that if the early, giant pyramids were *not* conceived and built as tombs but were designed to serve some other purpose, the implication then is that the evidence that consensus Egyptology holds up as proof of the tomb theory must, therefore, be wrong.

This is to say that somewhere along the nearly two hundred years of consensus Egyptology, some evidence has been completely overlooked while, at the same time, of the evidence that Egyptology *has* considered, a series of wrong interpretations have been made, resulting in flawed opinions and an incorrect paradigm emerging. But if the early, giant pyramids were *not* conceived as tombs (as some early texts indicate), then the implication is that they served some other purpose, and that, as such, behooves us to make a closer analysis of the key evidence that is presented in support of the tomb theory.

In this chapter a number of facts will be presented that, while not conclusively disproving the pyramid tomb theory, nevertheless raise some pertinent questions that ultimately place the theory in a more questionable light. At the very least, these ten facts will show that, of the evidence Egyptology has actually considered, the interpretation it has arrived at is, at best, highly contentious and there may exist a more plausible and better interpretation of this key evidence. These facts are presented in no particular order and arise from a number of sources that include the physical, logistical, practical, functional, and mythical.

In consideration of these ten facts it is assumed that each will be internally consistent with the culture and beliefs of the ancient Egyptians, will agree with the extant evidence that is currently available to us, and will not present an affront to simple logic and good common sense—the ultimate test of any theory. It should be noted, however, that the ten facts presented here are by no means exhaustive and that there are many other facts and/or issues that also cast doubt on or otherwise contradict the pyramid tomb theory that are not presented in this chapter. So, let us begin.

1. PYRAMID SIZE

The very first pyramids built by the ancient Egyptians were among the largest pyramids that they ever built over their more than three-thousand-year history. Indeed, the Great Pyramid of Khufu, believed to have been built circa 2550 BCE, was the tallest man-made structure in the world until the construction of the Eiffel Tower in 1889. The question that arises here is why did the ancient Egyptians suddenly depart from the construction of relatively low *mastaba* tombs made of crude mud-brick to the construction of truly monumental pyramid structures of dressed stone?

Egyptologists point to what they perceive as an evolution from mastaba to step pyramid to true pyramid but fail to adequately explain *why* such a radical transition was deemed necessary, why giant pyramids were suddenly needed when the simple "pit-and-mound" mastabas, shaft tombs, and rock-cut tombs were sufficient and had been the burial traditions of the ancient Egyptians for hundreds, if not thousands, of years? Why suddenly did the king apparently require a "ladder" (i.e., a large stepped pyramid) on which he could ascend to the gods? Why did the king suddenly desire to ascend to the heavens on a smooth-sided true pyramid that, if we are to accept the opinion of Egyptology, supposedly mimicked the rays of the sun, when such a device was obviously completely unnecessary prior to the arrival of the pyramid? This sudden need for a really tall structure (i.e., the pyramid) to assist the king's soul up into the heavens is all the more baffling given that the king's *ba* (a part of the king's soul) could actually *fly* up to the heavens of its own accord because it had wings.

Some commentators have argued that the pyramid was built so massive in order to reflect the greatness of the king, to satisfy the king's ego. This is somewhat improbable given that not a single official inscription bearing a king's name has ever been found inside any of the early, giant pyramids—not one. Neither have any statues of any king been found inside these pyramids. Indeed, the only statue ever found of Khufu—the builder of the Great Pyramid—stands a mere three inches tall and was uncovered at the ancient royal burial site at Abydos, far from his pyramid at Giza. Had these pyramids been built to satisfy the vanity of kings, as some propose, then it is not unreasonable to expect that such vanity would surely have found the names of these kings inscribed all over them—inside and outside—along with a preponderance of massive statues in the king's image. Such is the nature of vanity.

Furthermore, were these massive constructions simply reflections of massive egos, there is little doubt that Khufu, having had first bite of the Giza plateau cherry, would undoubtedly have built his pyramid on the high, imposing, and prestigious ground at the center of the plateau and not at a relatively low corner on the edge of the plateau. By so doing Khufu would have securely closed the door on the possibility of any future king trumping his own architectural marvel. In addition, by selecting the central, high ground of the plateau Khufu would also have benefited from the natural causeway that ran from the Nile up to the central high ground and would have saved himself the not inconsiderable headache and expense of having to build a massive artificial causeway deep into the Nile Valley. But concerns of prestige, of finance, and of potentially being upstaged seem not to have influenced Khufu's choice in the slightest, as clearly can be seen by his decision to reject the prestigious, central high ground with its advantageous natural causeway and, instead, to opt for the lower, northeast corner of the plateau, right on the cliff face, for the construction of his Great Pyramid.

And were these colossal structures built to reflect the greatness of the king (i.e., to satisfy his ego), then there is little doubt also that Menkaure, the builder of the smallest of the three main pyramids at Giza, would more likely have chosen a virgin site for his pyramid rather than have its relatively diminutive stature highlighted by its two illustrious predecessors standing high and mighty on the Giza plateau. By building away from Giza at a virgin site, Menkaure could easily have avoided such unflattering comparisons being made. But no, Menkaure was quite content to build at Giza, in the shadow of the two giant pyramids already there. So, as far as ego is concerned, the very placement of these monuments squarely contradicts such a motivation.

Other commentators have suggested that the pyramid evolved from the mastaba in order to provide greater security from robbers in a similar way that the mud-brick mastaba developed from simple pit-and-mound graves that would quickly erode away, revealing the tomb that would then be ransacked by people and animals. But given that the pyramids were built by people who knew how to cut, move, and stack huge blocks of stone from a quarry to build a pyramid, it would not have been lost on the king or his advisors that the very same people could do precisely the reverse to dismantle and gain access to his pyramid. Certainly the pyramids—were these truly tombs of kings—would have had guards and a priestly cult protecting them from being plundered, but often these were the very people the king had to fear the most. In this regard, a giant stone pyramid offered no more protection than the much smaller mastaba or rock-cut tomb.

Given the importance in the ancient Egyptian religion of preserving the king's mortal remains from desecrators and tomb robbers, building a tomb the size of a giant pyramid would have served only to act as a beacon, advertising for miles around the precise whereabouts of the tomb to those morally challenged individuals who would do it and the king harm. This situation seems all the more puzzling given that Khufu clearly understood the first principle of ensuring a secure and permanent burial: you create an underground tomb and you do not mark its location. We know that Khufu understood this basic principle because he buried his own mother, Hetepheres I, in such an unmarked tomb, one hundred feet underground at Giza. This tomb was only discovered by a freak accident in 1925, having been undisturbed and undiscovered for almost 4,500 years.

This raises the obvious question: If Khufu understood the best means to secure a safe and permanent burial (for his mother) with the use of a completely invisible, unmarked, underground shaft tomb, why then would he go against his own better judgment and build for himself the most highly visible tomb imaginable? As a secure and inconspicuous tomb, Khufu's Great Pyramid would have completely failed. For Khufu to have believed that such a massive structure could function as a secure and permanent burial site against tomb robbers contradicts his own common-sense actions with regard to his mother's new underground tomb, a tomb he built specifically underground and unmarked because her previous tomb had been found and robbed. And, it has to be said, common sense would have been as available to the ancient Egyptian culture as it is to our own.

In summary, if, as Egyptology asserts, the early, giant pyramids were conceived and built as eternal tombs for the kings of the period, then it seems that these monumental constructions were set in motion not for reasons relating to religion, nor to security or to vanity. It seems that there was some other, as yet unknown, motivation for the sudden introduction of these massively visible structures.

2. PYRAMID SHAPE

Without exception, the superstructures of mastaba tombs in ancient Egypt were always *rectangular* in shape, a tradition that stretched far back into antiquity, even in ancient Egyptian times. Curiously though, almost without exception, the pyramids of ancient Egypt were built *square;* that is, with their bases being regular quadrilaterals. There are only two exceptions to this, the first being Menkaure's pyramid (G3) at Giza, which, according to Lehner's measurements, is fractionally rectangular, with its north-south axis marginally longer than its east-west axis. (The reason for this will be discussed with fact 6, "Preconceived, Unified Planning.") The second rectangular pyramid is the very first pyramid ever built, the step pyramid at Saqqara attributed to Djoser, which again is marginally rectangular in shape. However, it is known that the construction of the step pyramid actually began with it as a square, and it was later modified to become slightly rectangular. Its eastern side was extended marginally in order to cover over and make secure eleven shaft entrances to the vast storage galleries beneath this pyramid.

But this raises a question: Why would the ancient Egyptians suddenly abandon an ancient tomb-building tradition of low, rectangular superstructures (i.e., mastabas) for their kings and queens in favor of giant, square superstructures (i.e., pyramids), and why would they *continue* to construct low, rectangular mastaba tombs and shaft tombs during the pyramid-building age (and long afterward) for every other royal or noble? In short, the square pyramid fundamentally contradicts the ancient Egyptian tradition of rectangular burial mounds, vis-à-vis the mastaba, a burial structure that the ancient Egyptians used for almost all of their history.

Furthermore, the burial chambers within the mastaba tomb (from which the pyramid supposedly evolved) were always deep underground, whereas the chambers within the pyramid were mostly either at ground level or high above ground level, thereby contradicting the ancient Egyptian axiom of "body to the earth, spirit to the sky." Accepting the further axiom that "form follows function," then this suggests that the square form of the pyramid served a different function to the rectangular form of the mastaba.

The question arises then: If the pyramids were not built as tombs then where are the bodies of the kings from this period to be found? Well, given the importance of the king's role in death during the Old Kingdom period, it would naturally have been of paramount importance to protect the king's remains from looters and desecrators, and the best way of achieving this would naturally have been to have the remains placed in an unmarked tomb, deep underground, similar to the tomb that we know Khufu created for his mother, Hetepheres I, at Giza.

Intriguingly, there are two kings from this early period who had built pyramids and whose names have also been found on mastaba tombs. Egyptologist J. P. Lepre explains, "The Third Dynasty Pharaoh Huni built a sizable pyramid at Maidum, but it did not contain a sarcophagus. Yet a quite large mastaba located 275 miles to the south at Bet Khallaf did in fact contain a granite sarcophagus, within which were the total skeletal remains of a large man. This mastaba contained the royal name of Huni."[2]

Lepre also goes on to further state that a mastaba tomb bearing the name of Djoser, the Third Dynasty king and builder of the step pyramid at Saqqara, had also been found. In relation to this, a mummified foot found in the so-called burial chamber of the step pyramid at Saqqara, which some believed to be the remains of Djoser, has been radiocarbon dated to (at least) one thousand years *after* Djoser's reign, indicating an intrusive burial in this structure.

And so we must ask: If these mastaba tombs bearing the names of Huni and Djoser were actually their true burial sites, what then was the purpose of the pyramids that Egyptology attributes to these kings?

3. PROVINCIAL PYRAMIDS AND CENOTAPHS

The Provincial Pyramids are a series of seven small step pyramids situated along the banks of the Nile for most of its length. These small pyramids, which consensus Egyptology attributes to Huni, have neither internal nor external chambers of any kind, nor are there any ancillary structures such as chapels, temples, or causeways associated with them. The Provincial Pyramids represent something of a mystery to Egyptologists, but there is one thing that is absolutely certain about these small pyramids and on which Egyptologists are agreed: they categorically were *not* built to function as tombs.

Similar to the Provincial Pyramids are the pyramids that Egyptologists believe were built not as *actual* tombs but as cenotaphs, or false tombs. These cenotaphs appear identical in most every way to other pyramids that Egyptologists *do* regard as tombs, except they were not intended for burial but were merely built as symbolic tombs. And, just as in the pyramids that Egyptologists believe were *real* tombs, no body of any king or any funerary equipment has ever been found inside any of the false tombs.

So here we have two pyramid types—some small, some large—that were built by the ancient Egyptians and that Egyptologists freely acknowledge were never intended for burial of any sort. Given the fact that neither the Provincial Pyramids nor the cenotaph pyramids were ever intended as tombs, in the absence of any primary evidence, surely the wonder must be that any Egyptologist can assert with any authority that *any* pyramid was ever intended for the purpose of royal burial.

4. MULTIPLE PYRAMIDS

Related to the issue of the cenotaph pyramids are those pyramids constructed by Sneferu—four in total (three giant pyramids and at least one of the small Provincial Pyramids, the one at Seila). Why would a king require *four* pyramids, three of which were truly massive?

The conventional view assumes that Sneferu desired to build a "true pyramid"; that is, a pyramid with perfectly smooth, sloping sides as opposed to the earlier step pyramid structures. This assumed objective of Sneferu is based on the simple fact that Sneferu didn't build any more pyramids after finally succeeding in building the world's first true pyramid, the Red Pyramid at Dahshur. But the fact of the matter is, we simply will never know if Sneferu would have gone on to build any more pyramids, because he died shortly after completing the Red Pyramid.

And then there's the fact that Sneferu's first "failure," the pyramid at Meidum (which some Egyptologists attribute to Huni), was later converted by Sneferu into a true pyramid. So we have to ask: Why did Sneferu need the later Red Pyramid when he obviously could have finished the Meidum pyramid as a true pyramid the first time around? In fact, after his first large pyramid "failure" at Meidum, Sneferu went on to build a second "failure" known as the Bent Pyramid. Conventional wisdom has it that it became apparent to Sneferu's builders after constructing about two-thirds of this pyramid that its slope angle was much too steep, and so the top third had to be given a shallower incline if it were to be completed safely and not collapse under its own weight. This resulted in the famous bend at the top of this pyramid.

But here's the thing: if Sneferu had desired a perfect, true pyramid from the outset, as Egyptologists insist, then clearly the Bent Pyramid was *never* going to satisfy this particular desire. So why then did Sneferu continue to complete this wholly imperfect and undesirable pyramid far beyond its point of "failure"? Sneferu could simply have halted the construction when the problem became known, stripped down the Bent Pyramid, and used the stone from that failed structure to start a new attempt at a true pyramid (assuming that was indeed his goal), and he could have done so secure in the knowledge that he already had a pyramid tomb standing by at Meidum that could be converted to a true pyramid at any time should he die prematurely and be unable to complete his mission.

That Sneferu went on to complete the Bent Pyramid far beyond its point of failure—including fitting casing stones and constructing a causeway and a temple—strongly suggests that the construction of a true pyramid was probably not the only goal of this king and that it seems also to have been Sneferu's aim to build as many pyramids in his lifetime as he possibly could, albeit some better than others.

All of which begs two obvious questions: Why would an ancient Egyptian king require four (or more) pyramids, and why would he set out to build as many pyramids in his lifetime as he possibly could? If we assume one of these structures was intended as an actual tomb, why would an ancient Egyptian king require two (or three) spare tombs? Does this make sense? Or is there something much more fundamental that we are misunderstanding about the true nature and function of these structures given that so many were built by just *one* ancient Egyptian king?

5. ANONYMOUS CHAMBERS, NAMELESS SARCOPHAGI

According to Egyptology, relatively few mastaba tombs from the Old Kingdom period or the sarcophagi placed therein were decorated or inscribed, although it is often the case that the chapel attached to the mastaba was usually inscribed with the deceaseds' names and titles (which is how Egyptologists have been able to piece together much of the family history of this period). While this observation is generally true, it seems that Khufu's family went a stage further whereby his offspring (including Crown Prince Kawab, who actually died *before* Khufu) were placing inscriptions (their names and titles) on their actual *sarcophagi* placed within the mastaba tomb.

Egyptologists speculate that the so-called mortuary temples built onto the pyramids were the equivalent of the chapels attached to the mastabas and that in these places the king's names and titles would have been inscribed. Alas, however, few pyramid mortuary temples (or valley temples) have survived, thus any evidence of inscriptions of the kings to

Figure 3.1. Sarcophagus of Kawab (son of Khufu) with inscriptions, Cairo Museum

whom Egyptology attributes the various pyramids is also unavailable. And those fragments that have been found in the area of the pyramid temples cannot be guaranteed to have originated there.

All of which raises the obvious question: If Khufu's offspring (including those who died *before* Khufu) were having their names and titles inscribed directly onto their sarcophagi, why do we find Khufu's supposed sarcophagus within his pyramid tomb completely devoid of such official inscriptions? Why didn't Khufu follow this "family tradition" and have his own sarcophagus inscribed with his names and titles?

As stated, Khufu's eldest son, Kawab, believed to have been the crown prince, died quite young and certainly before Khufu. We find that both his chapel and sarcophagus are inscribed.

An inscription in the doorway of Kawab's mastaba reads, "Her son, her beloved, Ka-wab, the daughter of her god, she who is in charge of the

Figure 3.2. Sarcophagus of Meresankh II (daughter of Khufu) with inscriptions, Museum of Fine Arts, Boston

affairs of the jmAt,* Meritites, his mother, who bore (him) to Khufu."[3]

Inscriptions are also found on the sarcophagus of Kawab within the mastaba tomb itself: "Priest of Selket, Kawab . . . the king's son of his body, Kawab . . . king's eldest son of his body, officiant of Anubis, Kawab."[4]

Likewise, the sarcophagus of Khufu's daughter, Meresankh II, is also inscribed with inscriptions that include her name: "King's Daughter of his body, Meresankh."[5]

And the sarcophagus of Minkhaf I, another son of Khufu, is also rendered with various offering inscriptions that also include his name. As noted in Wikipedia, "Minkhaf held the titles *Eldest king's son of his body, Chief Justice* and *Vizier* and these inscriptions, including his name, were found in four niches within the chapel of his mastaba tomb"[6] (italics added).

Clearly then, we see a pattern emerging here regarding the funerary arrangements of Khufu's children, at least one of whom died before Khufu himself. It seems to have been customary at this time to inscribe hieroglyphic inscriptions—including the deceased's name and titles—within

---

*"jmAt" is the transliteration from the original hieroglyphs. The word remains in its raw, transliterated form within this passage of text because Egyptology has not been able to interpret what this word actually means.

the adjoining mastaba chapel *and* directly on the sarcophagus that was placed within the mastaba tomb. In light of such contemporary evidence, it does seem somewhat peculiar that not a single official inscription of the deceased (name or titles) has ever been found in *any* of the chambers or on any of the sarcophagi of the early, giant pyramids of that era, including Khufu's Pyramid.

Conventional Egyptology would simply dismiss this anomaly as being down to the individual wishes of the various kings involved. However, this is to ignore a much greater issue here. Given the important role played by the dead king in ancient Egyptian society, the absence of the king's name anywhere in his supposed funerary structure, including his sarcophagus, presents a most peculiar and even dangerous situation. To understand why this is so requires a little understanding of ancient Egyptian religious thought.

To the ancient Egyptians, a person's soul was composed of nine different aspects or elements. While all aspects of the soul were important and interacted with each other, chief among these components were the *ka* (the life force), the *ba* (an individual's personality), and the *ren* (an individual's name).

Given that the afterlife at this early period of Egyptian history was reserved *only* for the king and given what we understand about the symbiotic relationship between the ba and the ren, it seems somewhat peculiar that—unlike some of the mastaba tombs of the time (including those of Khufu's children, as stated earlier)—we find no official hieroglyphic inscriptions of the reigning king's name or titles on *any* sarcophagi or in *any* of the early, giant pyramids that were supposedly built for these kings as their eternal tombs.

While it was believed that the ka would always remain with the body of the deceased within the tomb, it also was believed that the ba would fly away each day and return to the tomb, its eternal roost, each night, provided, of course, that it could find the correct tomb and mummy to return to. Were the ba to fail in returning to the deceased (for whatever reason), then the king would have been deemed to have died a second time, from which there was no recovery; the king's soul would be consigned to eternal oblivion, his blissful afterlife forever terminated, thus potentially plunging the kingdom itself into chaos, for the king would no longer be able to commune with the gods on behalf of his people to ensure their continued well-being.

To assist the ba in finding the correct tomb and mummy and in keeping with the ancient Egyptian axiom "He lives whose name is spoken," the name of the deceased would be inscribed on the walls of his or her tomb and/or on the sarcophagus itself. Inscribing the deceased's name in stone was to give the name permanence, that the name would become "*living words*." In this way the ba would know that it had found the correct tomb and be able to return safely to the correct mummy each and every night, thereby maintaining the king's place among the gods and safeguarding the future of the kingdom. Indeed, it was believed by the ancient Egyptians that to erase a person's name—including that of the king (a practice that became known as *damnatio memoria*)—would condemn the deceased's soul to eternal oblivion. In the online magazine *Egyptological,* Brian Alm writes:

> Of course, writing demarcated the elite from the rest of society, since it is likely that no more than 1% of the population was ever literate, but in these early times, long before the Afterlife was extended to non-royals, the exclusivity had a more profound meaning than just social standing. Writing would not be used to express ideas and narrative in a grammatical scheme until several centuries later; at this point the written word simply noted the names of things, especially—and very importantly—the names of people.
>
> The all-important name (*ren*) was associated with the furnishings of the tomb along with the tomb's owner: the deceased expected to take his treasures with him to his eternal home. The name, one of the nine aspects of being, or manifestations of the self . . . was a magical necessity of existence already acknowledged in the ontology of Predynastic times as a requisite for eternal life.[7]

Alm also showed the importance of the written word, especially names and titles, by including a photo of the Old Kingdom stele of Nefermaat from the Oriental Institute in Chicago, on which Nefermaat is proclaimed as "king's eldest son," "overseer of the works," and the vizier to Sneferu. The stele's text says, "He is one who made his signs in writing that cannot be erased."

And so it seems that for the king to enjoy an everlasting afterlife then his ba *must* be able to find the correct tomb and mummy each and every night—forever. It goes without saying, but the task of locating the correct pyramid tomb and mummy would have been made immeasurably easier for the king's ba with the simple inclusion of his name, inscribed as "living words" into the stone of the burial chamber and/or directly on the sarcophagus itself—as was done for the mastaba tombs and sarcophagi of Khufu's children.

It stands to reason then, that in the complete absence of such vital identifiers inscribed directly on the sarcophagi or within the burial chambers of these pyramids to assist the king's ba in locating his tomb and mummy, we have to give serious pause for thought and ask whether the early, giant pyramids could have successfully functioned as effective tombs for the kings of this period for whom they were supposedly built. And if the answer to that question is no, then we have to give serious consideration to the possibility that these early, giant pyramids might actually have been conceived and built to serve some other function altogether.

6. PRECONCEIVED, UNIFIED PLAN

Conventional wisdom asserts that each pyramid of ancient Egypt was designed as a single entity, a royal funerary complex, with little consideration given to what had gone before or would come after. In short, there was no grand, preconceived, unified plan for any of the pyramids—so we are led to believe. For Egyptology to ever concede that such a preconceived, unified plan is clearly exhibited in the early, giant pyramids would drive a considerable hole in the pyramid tomb theory, so it is perfectly understandable why Egyptology staunchly resists such notions.

In the previous chapter we observed how the first sixteen or so pyramids in ancient Egypt may have been designed to represent or may have come to represent the sixteen dismembered body parts of Osiris and, in their very placement on the Egyptian landscape, can be shown to resemble a crude outline image of the iconic Osiris figure. But there is considerably more to this grand, unified plan, and it is this second aspect of the planning that may well have been responsible for the association of the god Osiris with the constellation of Orion (i.e., the belt stars).

The three main pyramids at Giza are a prime example of such preconceived, grand planning. In chapter 1, it was stated how the layout of the three Giza pyramids is very similar to the pattern of the Orion's Belt stars, as proposed by Robert Bauval. What is not so well known is the more recent discovery that the relative proportions of each of the three main Giza pyramids can *also* be shown to derive—in a simple and systematic fashion—entirely from the pattern of the Orion's Belt stars shown in step 1 in figure 3.3a on page 66. The 16 steps that follow demonstrate the derivation of these proportions (figures 3.3a–3.3d).

Step 1. Plot the belt stars (Al Nitak, Al Nilam, and Mintaka) accurately on a blank sheet of paper.
Step 2. Extend a line (L1) between Al Nitak's center and Al Nilam's center.
Step 3. Double the length of L1.
Step 4. From the end of L1, extend a line (L2) to Mintaka's center.

For steps 5–8, see figure 3.3b on page 66.

Step 5. Double the length of L2.
Step 6. Box the L2 diagonal. We now have base B3.
Step 7. Mirror base B3. We now have base B3a.
Step 8. Replicate L1 and label it L3.

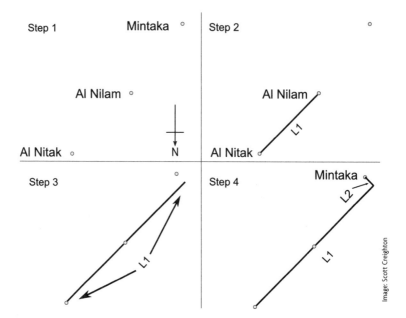

Figure 3.3a. Creating the relative proportions of the Giza pyramids from Orion's Belt, steps 1–4

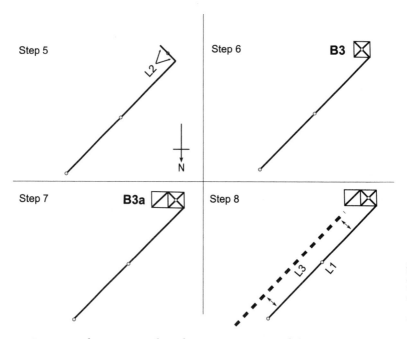

Figure 3.3b. Creating the relative proportions of the Giza pyramids from Orion's Belt, steps 5–8

For steps 9–12, see figure 3.3c on page 68.

Step 9. Place L3 through the diagonal of B3a.

Step 10. Remove B3a.

Step 11. Extend a line (L4) from the midpoint of L3 to Al Nilam's center.

Step 12. Double the length of L4.

For steps 13–16, see figure 3.3d on page 68.

Step 13. Box the L4 diagonal. We now have base B2.

Step 14. Extend a line (L5) from the endpoint of L3 to Al Nitak's center.

Step 15. Double the length of L5.

Step 16. Box the L5 diagonal. We now have base B1.

We have now produced the three-base (B1, B2, and B3) geo-stellar fingerprint for Orion's Belt (step 16). If we compare the relative proportions of these three bases with the relative proportions of the three Giza pyramids (G1, G2, and G3), we find that there is an extremely high agreement between the two sets of bases. It is worth noting here that were we to have commenced this design technique by drawing the initial line (L1) from Mintaka's center to Al Nilam's center we would have ended up with three entirely different bases that in no way match the relative proportions of the Giza pyramids. Only by starting the design with an initial line (L1) drawn from Al Nitak's center to Al Nilam's center can three bases be produced that relatively match the three Giza pyramids. This difference is important to understand, and its significance will be revealed in chapter 7.

For the moment, however, what is also significant about the above design method is that it requires the smallest of the Giza pyramids (the pyramid attributed to Menkaure, otherwise denoted as G3) to be designed *first* in order that the proportions of the other two Giza pyramids,

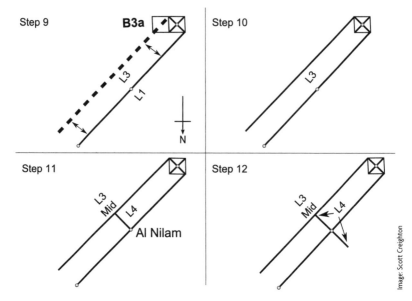

Figure 3.3c. Creating the relative proportions of the Giza pyramids from Orion's Belt, steps 9–12

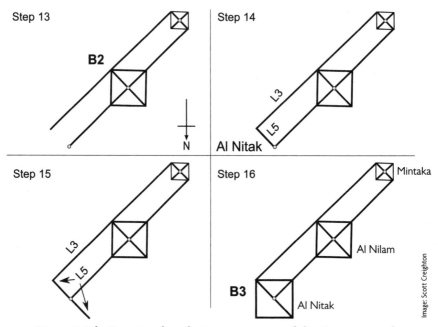

Figure 3.3d. Creating the relative proportions of the Giza pyramids from Orion's Belt, steps 13–16

G2 and G1, can then be determined. In other words, the *design sequence* of the geo-stellar fingerprint is the reverse of the actual *construction sequence* whereby, according to conventional Egyptology, G3 was built last, even though in the geo-stellar fingerprint of Orion's Belt, it is designed *first*. As such this constitutes a preconceived, unified design, a design, it should be said, that also includes the two crucial sets of three smaller satellite pyramids known as the Queens' Pyramids.

Furthermore, in using the Orion's Belt stars in this manner we find that B3 (G3's counterpart) will *always* result in a base that is very fractionally rectangular in shape on its north-south axis, while B2 and B1 (counterparts to G2 and G1) will be almost perfectly square. And, as pointed out earlier in this chapter, G3 is indeed very slightly rectangular on its north-south axis, as noted by Lehner, who wrote, "Menkaure's Pyramid was named 'Menkaure is Divine.' Smaller than his predecessors' pyramids at Giza, it has a base area of 102.2 × 104.6 m (335 × 343 ft)."[8]

Even today, using satellite mapping technology, we can observe the clear geometric relationship between the pyramids at Giza that is a natural outcome of the design method described above. We can easily observe at Giza how these structures are aligned along "inter-quarter lines" (figure 3.4 on page 70) that bisect the sides of these pyramids and their Queens' Pyramids. Such a geometric relationship is unlikely to be the result of simple, random design and placement of these structures.

That it can be shown that the relative proportions of the main pyramids at Giza can be derived simply and easily from the arrangement of the Orion's Belt star asterism is claimed by some as nothing more than coincidence. This is highly unlikely in the extreme. As stated in chapter 1, the Orion constellation, known to the ancient Egyptians as Sah, became the stellar personification of the ancient Egyptian god Osiris, the god of rebirth and regeneration who is associated with agriculture. In their 1994 book, *The Orion Mystery*, Robert Bauval and Adrian Gilbert show that the pyramids at Giza present an almost perfect match in their layout to the arrangement of the Orion's Belt stars. So here we have two quite separate correlations of the Giza pyramids with the Orion's Belt stars: their layout (i.e., belt asterism) *and* their relative proportions (i.e., belt geo-stellar fingerprint).

Now, the odds of such an outcome occurring by simple chance are somewhere in the order of trillions to one against. This is to say that if you were to create three random dots on a sheet of paper and ask a friend to create three random bases, to then find that the fingerprint created from your three dots matches the relative proportions, layout, order, and orientation of the three random bases drawn by your friend would be unlikely in the extreme. Yet, remarkably, such a highly unlikely occurrence is precisely what we have before us with the main pyramids at Giza. It is simply inconceivable that such an occurrence could result from simple random chance, so we have to conclude that Giza, contrary to what we are told by conventional Egyptology, is most likely the result of a preconceived, unified plan, a plan that also included the two sets of three Queens' Pyramids as the culmination markers of Orion's Belt (more on this in chapter 7).

If such a preconceived plan had been implemented then it is reason-

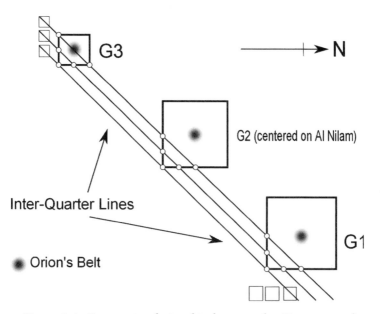

Figure 3.4. Geometric relationship between the Giza pyramids and their Queens' Pyramids

able to assume that the creation of the actual plan could have been conceived and put together very quickly—within days or even hours. Given that ancient Egyptian kings, according to the conventional view, did not plan the tomb of their sons or their grandsons and certainly not their sons' or grandsons' queens' pyramids, then such a preconceived plan to construct nine pyramids at Giza presents a significant obstacle to the conventional view of these structures having been constructed as tombs. And given that this plan (at Giza) would take around eighty years to implement, if they were conceived as tombs, how did the creator of the preconceived, unified plan know that eighty years into the future the king of that time (Menkaure) would only require three queen's pyramids? How would the designer of this preconceived plan have known that Khafre would not require *any* queen's pyramids (despite the fact that Khafre actually had five known queens—more than the other two Giza kings)?

The simple truth of the matter here is that the planner of Giza simply could not have known the future, ergo he could not have been designing these pyramids as tombs of kings and queens because he simply could not have known how many pyramid tombs to include in the plan. Yet the telltale signs of a preconceived, unified plan are clear for all to see, and in terms of probability, its existence is virtually beyond doubt. As such we have to conclude that the creator of this plan could not have been designing this set of pyramids at Giza (and by extension all other pyramids constructed before Giza) with the intention of the burial of future kings and queens, so we must further conclude that these structures were designed to serve some other purpose altogether.

7. PYRAMID SECURITY

Within the Great Pyramid of Khufu there are a number of curious features that permit us to question just how secure such a structure—were it to have been constructed as the king's tomb—would have been in fending off unwanted attention. As noted earlier in this chapter, the sheer physical size of the early pyramids would have attracted the attention of the unscrupulous for miles around. Remarkably, when these undesirables reached the Great Pyramid, it seems that its architect, far from making the structure impossible to breach, designed it in such a way as to practically *ensure* that it *could* be breached—not exactly the kind of thing a king seeking an eternal afterlife among the gods would remotely have sanctioned. There are a number of features of the Great Pyramid that lead us to this conclusion.

The Trial Passages

Slightly to the east of the Great Pyramid on the Giza plateau are a series of passages hewn out of the bedrock that run deep underground. The arrangement of these "trial passages," as they are known to Egyptologists, almost exactly replicates (on a much smaller scale) the internal arrangement of the passage system within the Great Pyramid, including the concealed Ascending Passage that leads to the upper chambers of the pyramid, including the supposed King's Chamber. In effect, the trial passages could be viewed as a map of the interior of the Great Pyramid, showing where to find and how to access the vital upper chambers within the structure.

The Descending Passage

The original entrance to the Great Pyramid was via a stone block that is believed to have swiveled open, revealing the long, unblocked Descending Passage. This narrow passage would take anyone who entered directly down to the lowest chamber known as the Subterranean Chamber. At around the halfway point down the long Descending Passage is the overhead junction of the Ascending Passage, and onward through the passage to the Grand Gallery lie the Ante Chamber and then the King's Chamber. We have to ask, however, why would the Descending Passage have been left unblocked?

When we consider how Khufu filled in the shaft entrance to his mother's underground tomb at Giza with rock-and-gypsum cement, we have to ask why this wasn't done for the tomb of the king. If this was to be the tomb of Khufu, it is simply inconceivable that Khufu would have permitted such easy access down this passage to allow intruders to attack the Prism Stone that once concealed the entrance to the Ascending Passage.

The Ascending Passage, the Granite Plugs, and the Prism Stone

As stated above, the entrance to the Ascending Passage was once concealed by a block of limestone known as the Prism Stone (now lost), and behind this an additional three massive granite plugs served to block this passageway. Given the estimated weight of the Prism Stone (several tons), manipulating it within the narrow confines of the passage system would have been virtually impossible, because it would have been physically impossible to deploy enough manual labor in this tight space for such an awkward and labor-intensive task. This has led some to argue that the Prism Stone was actually set in place *during construction* of the pyramid and, like the stone block at the entrance to the Descending Passage, perhaps swiveled open to allow entrance to the Ascending Passage. It has been calculated that the opening would have been around eighteen inches, making it difficult in the extreme for any funeral party with a bound mummy to pass through in any dignified fashion in order to reach the upper chambers for the final burial of the king.

It is further believed that the Prism Stone was set in place to camouflage the three granite plugs that were supposedly slid into place down the Ascending Passage (from their supposed storage location in the Grand Gallery) after the funeral party had squeezed themselves back out of the Ascending Passage through the narrow gap provided by the open Prism Stone. Because the passageways are mostly limestone constructions, anyone passing down the Descending Passage would immediately have noticed the different-colored granite plugs that blocked the entrance to the Ascending Passage, hence the need for the limestone Prism Stone that effectively covered the granite plugs, thus camouflaging the entrance to the upper passage system. If that was the case then we have to ask why the builders of the Great Pyramid simply did not block the Ascending Passage with large limestone blocks, thereby making it harder to distinguish them from the surrounding limestone structure. And why mark the location of the Prism Stone (thus the entrance to the upper passage system) on the floor of the Descending Passage? In this regard, one of the earliest pyramid explorers, the Astronomer Royal of Scotland Piazzi Smyth, wrote the following about the location marker, which was found by accident.

> Here, therefore, was a secret sign in the pavement of the entrance-passage, appreciable only to a careful eye and a measurement by angle, but made in such hard material that it was evidently intended to last to the end of human time with the Great Pyramid and has done so thus far.
>
> Had, then, that ceiling stone never dropped out at all, still the day might have come when the right man at last, duly instructed, would have entered the passage, understood that floor sign, and, removing the ceiling-stone opposite to it, would have laid bare the beginning of the whole train of those subaerial features of construction . . .[9]

Why would the builders create a "secret sign" on the floor of the Descending Passage, indicating the entrance to the Ascending Passage right overhead? Why leave such clues to assist in the discovery of the concealed upper passage system where, supposedly, the king's burial chamber was to be found? Surely such would have been the *last* thing Khufu would have wanted in his tomb since such markings would surely have invited inquiry, thus leading the intruder to investigate the right spots that would have inevitably led to the discovery of the upper passage system and the chambers beyond. As the tomb of Khufu, it is again quite inconceivable that such clues would have been set in place to assist an intruder.

Granite Plugs

As stated briefly above, beyond the Prism Stone blocking the lower end of the Ascending Passage are three granite plugs (still in situ), each

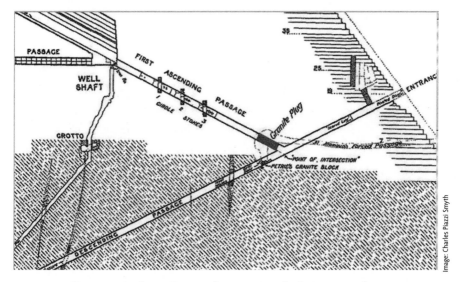

Figure 3.5. Great Pyramid passages with the granite plugs

weighing around five tons. Conventional thought asserts that these blocks would have been stored within the Grand Gallery and slid down the Ascending Passage after Khufu had been laid to rest in the King's Chamber at the top end of this passage system. The workers who pulled the release mechanism would then have made good their own escape via some unknown, secret passage system (presently believed to be the so-called Well Shaft) leading from the Grand Gallery to the unblocked Descending Passage. Of course, such an ancillary entrance completely bypasses and fatally undermines the granite plugs that were supposed to secure the tomb's main entrance passage.

But why were these unwieldy granite blocks even deemed necessary? As already mentioned, entrance to the pyramid could have been secured by simply blocking the Descending Passage with rock-and-gypsum mortar in the same manner that Khufu had sealed his mother's shaft tomb at Giza. And keeping in mind that all of this had to work the first time, how would the descent of these blocks into position within a gradually tapering passageway have been controlled and assured? In the words of Philip Femano, Ph.D.:

It is not conclusive that the builders chose to rely on the unpredictable behavior of gravity on two hewn and unpolished surfaces with different densities and coefficients of friction sliding along each other within a steep tunnel of carved block masonry, as their preferred method of securing a royal burial chamber. Likewise, it is not clear why the builders did not simply seal the pyramid at its main entrance on the north face, sliding the plugs from outside the pyramid into the initial, upper segment of the Descending Passage, capping the plugs with a casing stone, and dissuading anyone from entering the entire pyramid in the first place.

Unless one is to believe that the builders assumed ancient plunderers would stumble on the original entrance, crawl down the unremarkable Descending Passage to reach what appeared to be an "unfinished" Subterranean Chamber and be convinced that there were no other passages to plunder in the Great Pyramid, one is left to wonder why the builders allowed easy passage (or at least such an easy breach) down the Descending Passage at all.[10]

The Ante Chamber and the Portcullis Slabs

Having discovered the upper passage system (if by no other means then certainly via the clues left behind by the builders), the task for the intruders would then have been to work around the granite stones that blocked this passage (assuming, of course, that they had not discovered the secret exit used by the builders). Though difficult, this would not have been an insurmountable problem for a people who could quarry limestone and granite blocks of anywhere from 2.5 to 70 tons and maneuver them into place to construct a pyramid. If they could do that then it is not unreasonable to suggest that they could just as easily do the reverse by cutting around the much softer limestone.

Once entry into the Grand Gallery had been achieved, then the only remaining "security measures" protecting the King's Chamber were three portcullis slabs made of granite and set in place within the Ante Chamber, a small room just before the King's Chamber. But once

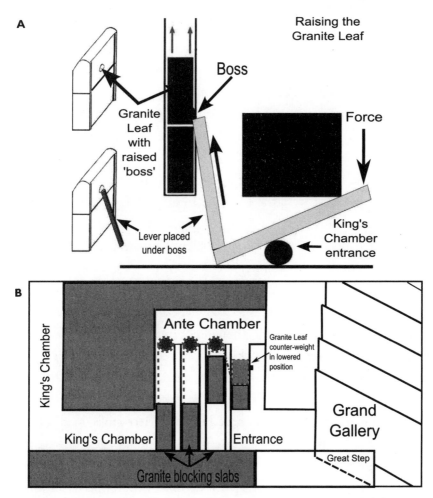

Figure 3.6. Ante Chamber portcullis system with Granite Leaf. (A) Shows the Granite Leaf being raised using a wooden lever under the "boss" (small stone protrusion), and (B) shows the Granite Leaf being used as a counterweight to raise one of the granite blocking slabs to the King's Chamber. Images by Scott Creighton. Image B based on Adam Rutherford original.

again, as if the builders went out of their way to assist an intruder, these granite slabs would have presented little resistance since the builders—rather conveniently—had left in place a fourth granite block known as the Granite Leaf (see figure 3.6). This stone, which is set into two grooves on either side of the Ante Chamber (akin to a sliding guillotine), could easily have been used as a counterweight mechanism with which to raise each of the three portcullis blocking stones, thereby allowing easy access to the King's Chamber.

So, once again we are left puzzled and perplexed as to why the builders would conceivably have left in place such a convenient and useful mechanism that would surely have assisted an intruder in gaining easy access into the heart of the pyramid. It is simply inconceivable that if this pyramid were the tomb of an ancient Egyptian king that such a mechanism would have been left in place to further assist anyone who might happen to reach the upper levels of the pyramid. For the builders to have left this counterweight stone intact is akin to a guard locking a bank vault and leaving the key in the lock. Simply removing this Granite Leaf after the King's Chamber had been sealed would have made it so much more difficult (though not impossible) for any intruder to then raise the portcullis blocking slabs. Yet the Granite Leaf counterweight was left in place and intact—the key left in the lock—and we have to ask why.

In summary then, what we have here is an accessible "map" of the Great Pyramid's interior passage system (the trial passages) outside the pyramid. We have easy access to the Descending Passage as it was never blocked. We have the camouflaged junction to the upper Ascending Passage conveniently marked on the floor of the Descending Passage. And we have an intact counterweight system to facilitate the raising of the portcullis blocks that were supposedly the final barrier to the King's Chamber.

Given all of this, one has to conclude that the ancient architects went out of their way to ensure that the Great Pyramid (and its internal chambers), although reasonably secure, was in no way as tightly secure as the builders *could* have made it; it is almost as though the builders were going out of their way to *invite* relatively easy access to whatever lay within.

8. INTRUSIVE BURIALS

Intrusive burials were part of a long tradition in ancient Egypt. Two such burials were discovered at Giza within G3 and G3b (Menkaure's Pyramid and one of his queens' pyramids). We have to ask: Why would such an intrusive burial be allowed to occur? Intrusive burial implies that an original burial was removed to allow for the intrusive burial to then take place. While these two acts may have been separated by a long period of time and completely unrelated to one another, it was the custom in ancient Egypt that if the body of the king was desecrated or otherwise destroyed by looters, then a ka statue could be made and placed within the tomb to serve in place of the original royal mummy that had perhaps been desecrated and/or removed. In this way the King's afterlife among the gods would be secured, as would the security of the kingdom. This religious belief and the facts that no original burial was found and that it was clearly considered permissible for someone else to use the pyramid as a tomb much later all strongly suggest that these pyramids had never actually been used as tombs in the first place.

9. QUEENS, BOATS, AND SOUL SHAFTS

Given that the afterlife in early Egyptian dynastic history was the reserve of the king and the pyramid was regarded as his "instrument of transfiguration and ascension" that would transform the king's ka and ba into an akh that could then ascend to the gods in the heavens, why then would pyramids have been constructed for Khufu's queens? Because it was not expected that the queens would receive such a soul transfiguration, why would it have been deemed necessary to build them an instrument of transfiguration; that is, a pyramid?

The same question can be asked of the boat pits around some of the Queens' Pyramids at Giza. If the afterlife was reserved for the king and his soul would journey through the Duat on a ritual vessel known as a solar barque, why were such features provided for queens when it was not expected that they would receive such an afterlife?

And what of the so-called star shafts of the Great Pyramid? If, as some authorities assert, the king's soul was intended to traverse these shafts in order that it could target its stellar destination and project itself in the right direction up into the starry heavens, why then would the king require several unassembled solar barques buried outside his pyramid? These unassembled boats were buried underground, while the internal soul shafts pointed skyward. Was it expected that the king's soul would come down from the heavens, having been projected there by the star shafts, to then embark on a solar barque on which to sail back up into the heavens? These mainstream ideas are somewhat inconsistent and seem to be at odds with each other and surely demand a more cohesive explanation.

10. THE SARCOPHAGI

Some of the key pieces of evidence Egyptologists hold up as proof that the early, giant pyramids were used as tombs for ancient Egyptian kings are the stone containers found within the internal chambers of a few of these early pyramids—stone containers that appear remarkably similar to the sarcophagi found in known mastaba tombs of the period. Appearances, however, can be deceptive.

First, while fragments of bone have been recovered from a number of the early, giant pyramids, only three pyramids from this period (G1, G2, and G3) contained a stone box, and of these none have yielded the remains of any ancient Egyptian king. As mentioned in chapter 2, a number of burials *were* found in some pyramids, but these are known to have been intrusive burials from much later times.

Second, a number of so-called sarcophagi have been found in modern times completely intact and unopened, having been undisturbed since first being placed in the chamber. When these stone containers were opened they were found to be empty. The conventional answer to this conundrum posited by Egyptology is that the king was perhaps killed in battle or that the body was otherwise unavailable at the time of burial. But this still does not explain why the supposed "sarcophagus" or "burial chamber" should have been found empty because, as stated previously, it is known that the ancient Egyptians in situations where the dead king's body was in absentia would fashion a ka statue of the king made of wood or stone and place this within the sarcophagus or within the tomb. We have to ask then: Why were no surrogate ka statues of the king found in these undisturbed "sarcophagi" or "burial chambers"?

There are further issues concerning these stone containers found in some of the early pyramids that raise further questions as to their true function, and these issues will be discussed in chapter 9.

It seems then that for the best part of two hundred years, consensus Egyptology has insisted that the early, giant pyramids of ancient Egypt were conceived and built as the eternal resting place of the deceased king and as his instrument of transfiguration and ascension that would carry him up to the heavenly realm and to his eternal afterlife. However, it is extremely difficult to reconcile the facts presented in this chapter with the overly simplistic and somewhat romantic and naive notions of the Egyptologists. There are simply too many anomalies, too many affronts to common sense, too many facts that simply do not fit the tomb paradigm that is so embraced by the Egyptologists.

Once again, however, this is not to say that the early, giant pyramids could not have been used as tombs at some point in their long history— of course they could. But it simply does not seem, from the available evidence and the facts presented here, that they could have been *originally* conceived and constructed with such a notion in mind, at least not at the beginning of the pyramid-building age.

If it is evidence that we must base our theories on, then the evidence presented in this book strongly suggests that these early, giant pyramids were not at all funerary in nature but seem to have been constructed with some other, grander purpose in mind, a purpose that seems to be associated with a chthonic ritual of "revivicating" the Earth.

4

Barriers to Discovery

I will reveal the secrets behind these doors.

ZAHI HAWASS

I had come so far on my journey of discovery only to find that, at the last gasp, I could go no farther, for stretching out before me—left and right for as far as the eye could see—stood a high wire fence (figure 4.1), a great barrier across the desert that had become known as "Zahi's Wall" after the former Egyptian head of antiquities, Zahi Hawass, Ph.D., who had instigated its construction. The "doorway" to my destination had been well and truly slammed shut and that, as such, meant there would be no great revelation or any ceremonial laying of my small, granite pyramid in honor of Osiris. The bitter irony of Hawass's words (in this chapter's epigraph) was not lost on me.

I couldn't believe I had come this far only to be thwarted at the final hurdle by such a hideous obstacle. My first thought was the obvious one: Why was such a barrier even necessary? Then I thought, Was it to prevent people getting out from the Giza site and into a restricted area, or was its purpose simply to prevent people from accessing the Giza site from the other side of this very long barrier? Or was there

Figure 4.1. "Zahi's Wall" blocks access to the Great Giza Triangle apex point location.

some other reason altogether? Was this fence perhaps erected to prevent anyone from getting too close to the very desert location I had identified, the apex point of the Great Giza Triangle? Was this theoretically significant location perhaps already known and being investigated by the Egyptian authorities, and was it now regarded as a restricted area, hence the construction of this barrier? Gaping through the wire fence I could see exactly where I needed to go—up and over a small hill about two hundred feet or so beyond the barrier. Frustration didn't even come close to what I was now feeling. I simply *had* to get beyond this insufferable obstacle.

I approached the fence to have a closer look, trying to see if there were any obvious gaps or weaknesses that I might be able to exploit. I trekked its length for about two hundred meters, back and forth, trying to find even the smallest weakness. But try as I might, the only thing I found was an abomination of twenty-first-century junk—sheets of newspaper, plastic bags, plastic cups, McD's wrappers, empty plastic water bottles, Coke cans, and a whole multitude of other undesirable refuse—all of it having been blown across the desert from the plateau, whereupon it had become snagged by the fence and had settled into a great drift of human garbage. Undoubtedly, archaeologists digging at this spot some five thousand years in the future will find it a most lucrative midden that will greatly assist them in their reconstruction of life in twenty-first-century Egypt.

Alas, however, not a single break was to be found in any part of the barrier.

Things were becoming desperate. I next thought about an attempt at climbing over the fence. It was high, as much as thirteen feet in places, and though it would most certainly be tricky, I didn't consider it by any means an impossible task. But then another thought crossed my mind. It might be electrified. There didn't appear to be any signs anywhere warning of this possibility, but then, this was Egypt; that there were no warning signs anywhere was no assurance of anything.

After some moments of anxious deliberation, I came to a decision. I'd come this far and to turn back now having been so close to my goal was quite unthinkable to me. The decision was made; I had to risk it.

I picked up a couple of Coke cans and threw them against the fence, whereupon they simply dropped to the sand with no apparent consequence. I wasn't quite sure exactly what I might expect to discover by doing this, but given that nothing obvious had occurred, I next (and very tentatively) extended a finger and tapped the wire fence, withdrawing my finger from the fence faster than a speeding bullet. No buzz. No spark. No "don't-even-think-about-it" tingling up my arm. Nothing. I gave the fence another quick tap, holding my finger on the wire just a fraction longer. Still nothing. It seemed to be okay.

So, with both hands I quickly grasped the fence and began a very precarious and mostly undignified ascent. Having perhaps reached a height of around four or five feet from the ground, it was then that something really bad happened. It was a noise—the most appalling, heart-stopping noise I had ever heard. I quickly let go of the fence, dropped to the ground, and glanced around in the direction of the noise. It had sounded like a horse or a donkey. But it wasn't. It was a camel, and atop the camel sat its rider, an Antiquities Guard, his dark, clouded face frowning at me, his automatic firearm resting casually across the saddle. Talk about being caught red-handed—like a kid with his hand in the cookie jar.

This was not good. I tried to say something, but the words came out choked and garbled. Thoughts of ancient legends and secret chambers melted from my mind like snow off a dike as I frantically tried to think of some way of dealing with this little crisis.

The guard said something in Arabic. I must have looked like a rabbit caught in the headlights, and the dumb look on my face surely told the guard that I wasn't from around those parts and that I hadn't a clue what he had asked me.

"Speak English?" he asked sharply. Somewhat sheepishly, I nodded.

"What are you doing out here? Where are you going?"

This was, of course, the very scenario I had built hope upon hope of avoiding. And here it was—bright as day and as real as your worst nightmare. But what could I say?

"I'm . . . I'm exploring." It was all I could think of that was vague enough and not an outright lie.

"Exploring?" He took a moment or two to swivel his head, side to side, scanning the length of the wall in both directions. "What exploring?"

Which was a fair enough question given that there was nothing at all of any obvious interest in this area to explore (other than the fence itself), and I could only answer him with another meek smile and a vague gesture with my arms flailing like windmills as if to say, "This place—Egypt." It wasn't the scorching heat that was now making me sweat buckets; it was more the looming thought of a dark and dingy Egyptian jail.

The guard considered my reply for a few moments. He was about to say something when a sharp burst of Arabic crackled from his radio. He picked it up and spoke into it, then returned it to his belt after a short exchange.

He leaned forward. "Where are you from? American?"

Again almost choking on the words, I spluttered, "No. Scottish. I'm from Scotland."

No sooner had I spoken than the guard leaned forward, his eyes grew wide, and his mouth becoming slightly agape. And then, as though I had just uttered a string of magic words, like a broken spell, the guard's hitherto menacing demeanor instantly changed.

"Scotland! Scotland! Then you are Egyptian, my friend," he proclaimed. "You are son of Egypt." He almost seemed to be rejoicing at this revelation, all of which I considered more than a little strange, but I was more than happy to accept the sudden change in the atmosphere between us. I beamed back brightly, though still not really knowing why the guard was so obviously elated by this revelation of my country of birth. I just kept on smiling.

"This we are taught as children at school," he announced. "Egyptians discovered Scotland many years ago in the old days. You are son of Egypt. We are brothers." He seemed very emphatic about that and certainly over the years I had read many of the ancient legends of how the Scottish (and Irish) people were believed to have originally descended from the land of the pharaohs. Indeed, even today, the Egyptian businessman and philanthropist Mohamed Al Fayed has plans under way to erect in his Highland estate of Balnagown in Scotland a statue of Princess Scota (sometimes given as Scotia), an ancient Egyptian princess who legend tells us had to flee Egypt with her husband and many of her followers, whereupon she traversed through Greece and the lands of the Mediterranean until, eventually, she reached Spain. From there Scota and her small band crossed over into Ireland, where they fought a bloody pitched battle, and finally, after a number of years, her people, the Scoti or Scots, finally crossed the Irish Sea and arrived in Scotland, which was so named in honor of the princess.

Indeed, of this connection of the Scots to ancient Egypt, Al Fayed writes:

Legend has it that over 3,600 years ago an Egyptian army sailed to a land north of Ireland and named it Scotland after their princess, Scota.

Does this mean that the kilt's origins are embedded in ancient Egyptian dress? Quite possibly. The origination of the kilt has had historians stumped. Some speculate that an Englishman introduced the Celtic kilt; some say it stems from the Irish; others suggest its roots are planted all the way back in Egypt. And there is evidence to support this last theory.

In the early 1440s a work called the "Scotichronicon" records Walter Bower writing of proof that the Scots were of Greek and Egyptian descent; not only that, but the country's name derived from the Egyptian Princess Scota.

Apparently, Scota sailed from Egypt to Ireland with her sons and an army, intent on avenging the death of her husband who had been killed at the hands of the Irish. She died on Irish soil and is said to be entombed in Gleann Scoithin, Kerry (now Foley's Glen). Some time later a group from Ireland called Scotis sailed north, settling in what became known as Scotland.

The discovery of two Egyptian sailing ships in a Yorkshire Estuary, dating to around 1400 BC supports this theory, as do other archaeological findings in Scotland, including Egyptian faience beads dating from the same period.

. . . It is probable then, that the Egyptian soldiers swapped their linen kilts and belts for a warmer woolen weave. What's more, when they sailed from Ireland to Scotland they took with them many native Irish words, including tarsna, meaning crosswise which later became "tartan." No under-garments were worn.[1]

I was aware also of other ancient traces that seemingly linked these two ancient nations. The Scots are renowned the world over for their kilt, which, as Al Fayed points out, was first worn by the ancient Egyptians. The ancient Scots also, just like the ancient Egyptians, mummified their dead and, just like the ancient Egyptians, knew the apex of the pyramid (a stone mountain) was capped with a *benben* stone, and so the ancient Scots (even to this day) refer to the mountains in Scotland as *bheins* or *bens,* as in Ben Nevis, Ben Lomond, and so on. Furthermore, recent scientific research into the DNA of Tutankhamun has reported the controversial (and disputed) discovery that a particular haplogroup of his DNA (R1b1a2) is found most predominantly within the DNA of the Celtic (Irish/Scottish) people. It is hoped that new DNA profiling techniques such as "next-generation sequencing" will produce more detailed and accurate information that might finally help settle this thorny question.

And finally, in Munster, County Kerry, in the southwest of Ireland there is a place formerly known as Glenn Scota (now Foley's Glen), where, according to Irish legend, Princess Scota fought a bloody battle against indigenous Irish tribes (the Tuatha de Danann) and was defeated and killed (see figure 4.2). As Egyptologist Lorraine Evans explains:

> The *Annals* then goes on to relate how forty-eight married couples, four servants and Scota, daughter of a pharaoh, accompanied the Sons of Mil across the sea from Spain when they went to seek land from Ireland. They proposed to take Ireland at Inbatr Slaine because of the prophecy that said a famous company would take Ireland at that place. . . . In this battle died Scota, daughter of a pharaoh, wife of Eremon.
>
> The Account of Scota's death at the battle of Slieve Mish is also confirmed in the *Lebor Gabala,* where it states that the sons of Mil originated from northern Spain. The fleet subsequently left Spain and sailed to Ireland to take it from the Tuatha de Danann. On the third day, after landing, they fought a bloody battle at Slieve Mish. In this battle fell Scota the daughter of a pharaoh. . . . The battle lasted for a long time, and the sons of Mil were eventually victorious and took the seat of Tara.[2]

Figure 4.2. Signpost to Scotia's (Scota's) Grave on the roadside, near Tralee, County Kerry, Ireland

Photo: Michael O'Carroll

"You are Egyptian," the guard said emphatically with a smile as wide as the Clyde.

"Yes, I suppose I am," I replied, smiling back and nodding affirmatively. Given the more relaxed atmosphere I felt brave enough to ask about the fence. "Why is this fence here?"

His response was very matter-of-fact. "It is to protect the monuments. And to protect the visitors. You must go from here. It is not safe to be out here alone."

The guard's remark was presented more as an order than a choice. I felt I had pushed my luck far enough that day and did not pursue my questions further. We said our farewells, and the guard remained at the fence, watching as I turned back in the direction of the road that would take me back to the Giza pyramids. It had not been a good day, but though bitterly disappointed at not reaching my goal, I figured that matters could have been a whole lot worse. But the thought remained in my head, Why the fence? Some time later I e-mailed Hawass to ask this question about his wall and received pretty much the same reason as the Antiquities Guard had stated to me: "The 'Wall' is there for the protection of our guests."[3]

Hawass did not elaborate on this, but shortly after my visit to Giza plans were hatched by him to revamp the wall, ostensibly to prevent "hawkers" from peddling their wares to tourists. As such, all manner of additional security features were added in order to foil the hawkers.

Egypt's famous Giza Pyramids are being given a £14m ($27m) makeover, starting with a state-of-the art security fence to stop hawkers harassing tourists.

Visitors to the World Heritage site have for years had to fend off persistent peddlers, offering camel rides and trinkets. Now a 12-mile (20-km) fence, complete with infra-red sensors, security cameras and alarms has been erected. It is the first phase of a project to modernize the 5,000-year-old site. Egyptian authorities say once the revamp is complete, it will make visiting the Wonder of the World a friendlier experience.

The chain-link fence with its motion sensors, which reaches a height of 13ft (4 metres) at some points, will set off alarms and alert the security control room if anyone gets too close. Watched by CCTV, visitors will now enter through a security building and pass through gates with metal detectors and X-ray machines.

The site where the three Giza Pyramids stand—located on the outskirts of the capital, Cairo—used to be completely open and tourists faced a gauntlet of peddlers selling everything from souvenir statues to photographs.[4]

CCTV, infrared sensors, motion detectors, metal detectors. When one considers that such security measures are not in evidence at any of the other large pyramid sites, this does seem a bit over the top if it truly is, as Hawass has stated, simply to prevent local people from trying to sell a few souvenirs to tourists—especially so when many of them actually peddle their wares *within* the Giza complex itself, having paid entry themselves to gain access to the site and all the tourists milling around there. It rather seems to me that there was another unspoken motive for having this additional security put in place at the Giza site. And it occurred to me that this motive may actually be more to do with preventing people from gaining access to restricted areas beyond the wall. As previously mentioned, Could the Egyptian authorities already know about this apex location, and have they perhaps already discovered something there, something that they are perhaps trying to keep under wraps?

For the moment, however, such questions would have to be set aside. I could go no farther in my quest, and so, as I wearily retraced my footsteps along the desert road, I resolved to return to my hotel and try to find some other means of getting beyond the wall and accessing the apex location in order to complete my journey, to give homage and offer my gift to Osiris. I had come this far and was not about to be beaten so easily. It was time to put Plan B into action.

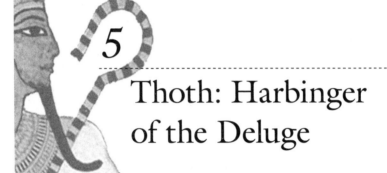

5

Thoth: Harbinger of the Deluge

The pyramids themselves, doting with age, have forgotten the names of their founders.

THOMAS FULLER

As I trekked back along the desert road, the three giant pyramids of the Giza plateau once more presented themselves to me in majestic fashion, the unified body of Osiris becoming more and more dismembered or disjointed with each and every step. From where I now stood the three great triangular forms appeared against the horizon almost like the sails of a great ship, sailing over the rolling sand dunes of the desert almost like waves on the sea—a group of pyramids known to the ancient Egyptians as Akhet Khufu (Khufu's horizon).

According to conventional Egyptology, Akhet Khufu is the name the ancient Egyptians gave to Khufu's Great Pyramid, although there has been much conjecture over the years as to what this term really means or, indeed, refers to. It is my contention that the name Akhet Khufu, contrary to mainstream opinion, actually refers to the *entire*

Giza site (not solely the Great Pyramid of Khufu) and that this some-what enigmatic ancient name has been misinterpreted by Egyptologists as meaning "horizon" but instead refers to the coming deluge antici-pated by the ancient Egyptians. In brief, the name Akhet Khufu, rather than meaning "Khufu's horizon," should more properly be translated as something like "protects [against the] coming deluge of Thoth."

As was touched on in chapter 1 of this book, a number of ancient legends associate the building of the early, giant pyramids—in particu-lar the Great Pyramid—with one of the earliest gods of ancient Egypt, Thoth (later paralleled with the Greek god Hermes). Typically the god Thoth is portrayed in the ancient Egyptian pantheon as the god of knowledge, writing, and science. In his anthropomorphic form, Thoth appears with the body of a man and the head of an ibis (figure 5.1), although he is sometimes portrayed in the form of a baboon.

In *Legends of the Gods: The Egyptian Texts,* British Egyptologist Sir

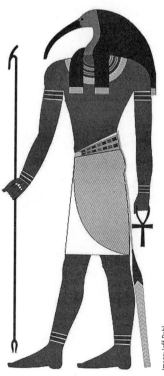

*Figure 5.1. Thoth, in one of his forms
as an ibis-headed man*

Image: Jeff Dahl

E. A. Wallis Budge writes of the relationship of Thoth with the ancient Egyptian god Ra and of the various forms Thoth could take.

> Thoth was to be his vicar, to fill his place, and "Place of Ra" was to be his name. He gave him power to send out a messenger (hab), so the Ibis (habi) came into being. All that Thoth would do would be good (khen), therefore the Tekni bird of Thoth came into being. He gave Thoth power to embrace (anh) the heavens, therefore the Moon-god (Aah) came into being. He gave Thoth power to turn back (anan) the Northern Peoples, therefore the dog-headed ape of Thoth came into being. Finally Ra told Thoth that he would take his place in sight of all those who were wont to worship Ra and that all should praise him as God. Thus the abdication of Ra was complete.[1]

How then did Thoth come to be associated in these legends with the Great Pyramid and other pyramids too? The following passage (previously presented in chapter 1 of this book) tells how the ancient Egyptians thought of the imminent flood that would destroy their civilization.

> Then Thoth, being the tongue of the Great God declares that, acting for the Lord Tem, he is going to make a Flood. He says: "I am going to blot out everything that I have made. This Earth shall enter into (i.e., be absorbed in) the watery abyss of Nu (or Nunu) by means of a raging flood, and will become even as it was in primeval time. I myself shall remain together with Osiris, but I shall transform myself into a small serpent, which can be neither comprehended nor seen." Budge explains: ". . . one day the Nile will rise and cover all Egypt with water, and drown the whole country; then, as in the beginning, there will be nothing to be seen except water."[2]

The passage above is believed by the ancient Egyptians to have been the words of the god Ra, although the words were actually spoken through the god Thoth (the "vicar" of Ra), thus Thoth, in speaking these words, is associated with the coming deluge, as the harbinger or messenger of the deluge.

This is not to say, of course, that the gods Ra and Thoth actually conspired to send a great deluge to destroy the ancient Egyptian kingdom. But to the ancient Egyptians everything, good or bad, was believed to be caused by the desires and the actions of their various gods. That the ancient Egyptian astronomer-priests went away and measured "the height of the stars" (as instructed by Surid) and found something abnormal about their disposition would have been regarded by them as the work of the gods. And the great future deluge they believed would arise as a result of the displacement of the heavens would also have been regarded as the will and work of the gods. And that they had even managed in the first place to obtain this knowledge of the abnormal state of the heavens would also have been deemed as wisdom that was bestowed on them by their great god of knowledge and wisdom, Thoth. In this sense, it can be seen how the god Thoth, by imparting knowledge of a future deluge to the king (via his astronomer-priests), would—by extension—become inextricably associated with the means by which the king hoped his kingdom could survive this anticipated calamity; that is, the construction of the pyramid arks.

In short then, while Thoth may not have been directly responsible as the *actual* builder of any of the pyramids, the wisdom that this god imparted to the ancient Egyptians—knowledge of a coming deluge—provided the motivation for these pyramids to be constructed.

But what evidence, if any, is there of Thoth's association with the Great Pyramid and what connection is there with this and an anticipated deluge? The evidence of such, in my opinion, has always been available to us and is right there in the very name the ancient Egyptians gave to the Great Pyramid and the Giza plateau—Akhet Khufu.

As stated at the opening of this chapter, to many Egyptologists the term Akhet Khufu is to be interpreted simply as meaning "Khufu's horizon," although this translation itself is bound up with many differing views among academics as to what "Khufu's horizon" actually meant or was. Most academics believe the term is connected with the idea of rebirth in that as the sun is reborn on the eastern horizon each and every day, so the Great Pyramid, as Khufu's (personal) horizon, would ensure the transfiguration and rebirth of the king each and every day. As Professor Jan Assmann writes:

> In Egyptian the pyramid of Cheops (whose Egyptian name was Khufu) is called akhet of Khufu. Akhet is the threshold region between the sky, the earth, and the underworld; in particular, akhet is the place where the sun rises. The etymological root of the word has the meaning of "blaze, be radiant"; likewise, the hieroglyph for akhet has nothing in common with the pyramid, but is a pictogram of the sun rising or setting between two mountains. The pyramid does not represent such an akhet, but symbolizes it in an aniconic way. The term of comparison between akhet and pyramid is the idea of "ascent to heaven." As the sun god ascends from the underworld to the akhet and appears in the sky, so the king interred in the pyramid ascends to heaven by way of his akhet, his threshold of light.[3]

This is, of course, all very symbolic and is only one of several attempts by scholars at interpreting the symbolic meaning of the name Akhet Khufu. The Egyptologists also tell us that it was further believed by the ancient Egyptians that the king's ba and ka (two aspects of the king's soul) would undertake some alchemical transfiguration into what is known as an akh and that this transformation was facilitated by and occurred within the pyramid. Egyptology further believes that the word *akh* is related to the physical horizon by virtue of the akh passing through the watery underworld known as the Duat (symbolically or otherwise) to emerge anew on the horizon, where the sun is reborn each and every day. It stands to reason then (according to the Egyptologists) that Khufu's akhet—his pyramid—must have been where his akh was created through some mysterious transfiguration of the king's ka and ba and rose forth as an "effective one" from within his own "personal horizon."

However, this interpretation of Akhet Khufu put forward by Assmann is all well and good except for the not-insignificant problem that the akhet pictogram for "horizon" (believed to depict the sun rising between two mountains; figure 5.2) did not actually exist when Khufu was building his Great Pyramid, as is implied in Assmann's quote above. Indeed, this pictogram only came into being around the end of the Fifth Dynasty, long after Khufu and the completion of the early, giant pyramids.

Notwithstanding this inconvenient fact, the early Old Kingdom of Egypt used, according to the Egyptologists, a different version of the word *akhet* (interpreted by many Egyptologists *also* as meaning "horizon"). The pictogram for this supposedly earlier version of the word *akhet* (horizon) is entirely different from the sun disc between two mounds and invokes instead the use of the ibis (see figure 5.4 on page 100), which has various translations, inter-alia, "intelligence," "illumination," "shining," "beneficial," and "useful."[4]

Lehner was probably one of the first academics to recognize the translation problem that these two quite distinct versions of the word *akhet* present. In Lehner's view the older term *akhet,* with the "crested ibis" (figure 5.4), should *not* be translated as "horizon" at all but instead is to be associated with the "spirit of Khufu." Lehner writes, "Joining the stars, the king becomes an akh. Akh is often translated as 'spirit' or 'spirit state.' It derives from the term for 'radiant light,' written with the crested ibis. . . . Akh is also the word for 'effective,' 'profitable,' 'useful.'"[5]

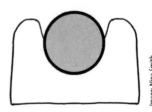

Figure 5.2. The akhet pictogram is believed to represent the sun rising between two mountains.

Image: Nina Smith

But it seems to me that even Lehner fails to properly grasp the precise nature of the term *akhet* (with the ibis glyph), for while the root etymology of the ibis glyph (*akh*) may well be associated in some way with "radiant light," as Lehner and other scholars believe, this should not necessarily or automatically imply that this "radiant light" is to be related to or interpreted as "spirit" or "spirit state" or "spiritual light"; there is another perfectly logical and contextually appropriate interpretation for the "radiant light" interpretation of this enigmatic hieroglyph.

Here then, through the use of the ibis hieroglyph, in the earliest version of the name Akhet Khufu, we find the first tangible link of the Great Pyramid to the ancient Egyptian god Thoth, who, as stated at the beginning of this chapter, is often depicted by the ibis. But how then is the ibis connected with the concept of a coming deluge, and, more specifically, how can the ibis (akh) be logically and contextually associated with the various interpretations of "intelligence," "illumination," "shining," "beneficial," and "useful" that Lehner and other academics believe is to be associated with the term *akh*?

If the translations given above of the ibis glyph (akh) truly means "intelligence," "illumination," "effective," and so on, then, in terms of an anticipated deluge, it is possible that we can understand how the ibis bird "illuminates" not so much with "radiant light" or "spiritual light" but rather with the *light of wisdom*.

In ancient Egypt the ibis was regarded as an "enlightened" bird blessed with the wisdom of Thoth, a wise bird that "heralded the inundation" (of the Nile). As such, it is my opinion that the ibis should not be regarded so much as "shining" in the sense of radiance like the sun or a star (thereby wrongly associating it with "spiritual light" and, by extension, the pyramid as tomb), but rather with the "radiance" or "illumination" that we would today attribute to a clever or wise person (i.e., a "bright spark" or an "enlightened one"). In short, the ibis (akh) need not be regarded as "spirit light" but rather as "one that illuminates with its wisdom."

So if the Arab chroniclers are correct in telling us that the early giant pyramids were built as arks to protect against an imminent deluge, then it seems that the very name of the Great Pyramid—Akhet Khufu—is, through the use of the ibis in this name, inextricably associated with the knowledge of a coming "deluge" or "inundation" spoken by Thoth, himself symbolized by the ibis. In short, the use of the ibis in the name of the Great Pyramid, Akhet Khufu, alludes to foreknowledge of a coming inundation.

Now, just to add some further intrigue, it so happens that there is yet another ancient Egyptian word *akhet* (spelled the same way) that actually means "time of the flood" or "flood season," although this version of *akhet* is generally believed to be associated only with the annual Nile inundation and not the cataclysmic deluge spoken of by Thoth.

But we can easily determine the difference between the normal, annual inundation of the Nile and the anticipated catastrophic deluge. To recognize this difference requires an understanding of the very basics of ancient Egyptian hieroglyphics.

Ancient Egyptian hieroglyphics employ a series of signs to impart meaning but also to phonetically spell out a word. These signs could be written horizontally left to right or right to left, or even vertically. When written horizontally, the signs are always read from the direction in which an animal or person is facing. When reading signs in a vertical column, they are always read from top to bottom. As with any language there are little quirks and exceptions to the general grammatical rule, but we need not concern ourselves with such complications; we need only the basics here.

The second important thing to understand is that ancient Egyptian hieroglyphs did not employ vowels but used only consonants, although signs for some vowel sounds would be developed much later in ancient Egypt. This means that the word for "horizon" (*akhet*) would be written as "kh t," and the word for "flood season or flood period" (*akhet*) would *also* be written as "kh t." (Note: although *kh* is two of our Western letters, phonetically it represents just one sound that is pronounced "ch," as in "Bach.") Of course, the ancient Egyptians did not use our alphabet; they had their own phonetic alphabet, which used signs (or multiple signs) that represented specific sounds (phonograms).

The two images in figures 5.3 and 5.4 show the hieroglyphs for *akhet* (flood season) and *akhet* (horizon).

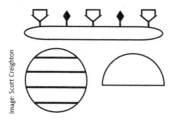
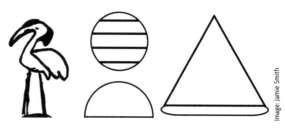

Figure 5.3. *Akhet (flood season)*   Figure 5.4. *Akhet (horizon)*

We can see from figures 5.3 and 5.4 that they have three signs in common—the disk with the crossed lines (*kh*), the half circle (*t*) and the ellipse (marsh or flooded land glyph), which has no phonetic sound value in this instance. Many words in ancient Egyptian writing were represented by a single sign known as a logogram (or ideogram), which represented the general idea of the word. However, because it was almost impossible to represent abstract ideas with a single sign, ancient Egyptian scribes would use phonograms to assist the reader in determining the correct word. A phonogram is a sign that corresponds to a specific phonetic value (i.e., sound), and multiple phonograms could be used to spell out the word.

However, as stated, because the ancient Egyptians did not use any vowels in their writing, this resulted in many words having very similar spellings, so in order to clarify the specific meaning of a particular word the scribes would add additional signs known as "determinatives" to the end of a word where needed, thus giving the general context of the particular word. To understand this basic concept, let us consider the following example using our modern Western alphabet. Try to identify the word in figure 5.5.

It is quite impossible to know the intended meaning of the word in

r n

Image: Scott Creighton

Figure 5.5. What is this word?

Figure 5.6. The cloud logogram symbolizes RaiN.

figure 5.5 because, without vowels, we are not able to read the two letters as a word. It could be *run, rain, ruin, urn,* or many others. To help identify the specific word intended, the Egyptian scribes would often present a clue in their writing to make the word clear. This clue might be a logogram at the beginning of the word (or when required, a determinative at the end of the word) to symbolize the general idea of the word.

With the inclusion of a logogram (the cloud symbol) in the above example we can now understand exactly how the word is to be interpreted—as "rain." (Note: while logograms at the beginning of the word have phonetic values, determinatives at the end of the word do not and are completely silent. In the example in figure 5.5, the cloud sign would have the phonetic value "r," which would then be spelled out with the phonetic compliment "r.")

So far, so good. In figure 5.3 we have the logogram for a marsh or flooded land with crops growing from it. This logogram on its own provides us with the idea of the land (the oval glyph) being covered with water to enable crops to emerge from the land. This is a reasonable logogram to symbolize the seasonal Nile inundation. This logogram is then reinforced with the signs of "kh" and "t" (the hatched circle and half-circle) to phonetically spell out the actual word *akhet.* Thus we have *kh t* or *akhet,* meaning "flood season" or "time of flood."*

---

*The vowels represented in ancient Egyptian words such as *kh t* (*akhet*) are added by modern scholars purely for convenience. Theoretically the ancient Egyptian word we write as "akhet" might actually have been spoken by an ancient Egyptian as "ukhoti" or "eekhita" or some other variation. We have simply no way of really knowing what vowels were employed by the ancient Egyptians or how their words actually sounded, so modern scholars developed a fairly arbitrary convention to insert vowels into Egyptian script to facilitate its pronunciation.

Let us turn now to the second akhet image (figure 5.4), with the ibis. The signs are to be read from left to right, and where signs are placed one above the other, these should be read from top to bottom. As stated earlier, according to Lehner, the first sign—the crested ibis—presents a logogram for the idea of "spirit" or "spirit state," or something along those lines. The hatched circle sign (*kh*) and the half-circle sign (*t*) give *kh t*. But in this version of akhet we do not find the flooded land logogram with crops emerging from the floodwaters, which would indicate the annual flood season but are instead presented with the ibis logogram. So logically this word *kh t* with the ibis logogram *must* have a different meaning than the seasonal "Nile inundation." It is not unreasonable to suggest that with the ibis logogram what is being alluded to here is an inundation but an inundation of a quite different kind.

As previously stated, the ibis logogram is given the phonetic value "akh." Once again it is spelled with the hatched-circle sign ("kh") and the half-circle sign ("t"). Thus we have the word *akhet*. The additional sign of the strip of land with the pyramid on top is offered as a determinative to assist in the understanding of the word (the context) and has no phonetic value. It is believed that the strip of land glyph (some translations say "island") is associated with "horizon," while the pyramid glyph is believed to symbolize the tomb where the akh ("effective one") is created.

It has to be said that the conventional understanding of this version of the word *akhet* as meaning "horizon" seems to be something of a tortuous and convoluted interpretation. We might well ask: How exactly does the crested ibis as a logogram easily and obviously convey the idea of "spirit" or "radiant light" (akh)? As previously stated, the basic concept of the logogram is that the sign itself should symbolize the idea of the word and that it should do so in as clear, simple, and unambiguous a fashion as possible. The use of the ibis as a logogram to symbolize "spirit" or "radiant light" is beyond a stretch, and these are not concepts that are at all easily conveyed with the use of such a symbol. Indeed, the idea of "radiant light" or "spirit" could have been better and more

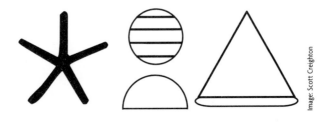

Figure 5.7. Akhet as "spirit" would be better conveyed with a star symbol.

obviously conveyed with the use of a star sign (also known as an akh; see figure 5.7).

The rendering of *akh* using a star logogram rather than an ibis logogram would make much more sense since a star is associated with light in a very clear and obvious way, and furthermore, it was believed by the ancient Egyptians that the king's spirit would ascend to the starry realm via his pyramid to become a star (a god) himself.

So, we have to ask again: Why the use of the ibis to represent the abstract concept of akh (i.e., "effective spirit of light") and not a star, which would have more clearly conveyed such an abstract idea? Is it possible that the crested ibis has been wrongly interpreted by the Egyptologists as meaning "spirit" and that this logogram might have some other meaning altogether?

And notice also the pyramid sitting atop the glyph for marsh or flooded land; why are these signs used as a determinative in this version of *akhet*? What idea are the pyramid and flooded-land as determinative signs trying to convey here? Could it be that the pyramid and flooded-land glyphs in this version of *akhet* are actually conveying the idea of the reemergence of the land from the coming deluge of Thoth (symbolized with the ibis), just as it had occurred in the earliest ancient Egyptian creation myth, and from that original mound (represented by the pyramid sign) everything in creation came forth?

Well, we know that the word for "time of flood" (akhet season) uses the phonetic complements of "kh" and "t," so might not this term be used along with the ideogram for the crested ibis to *also* mean "time of flood," but a different kind of flood?

It rather seems to me that the early interpreters of the word *akhet* with the crested ibis were too quick to want to associate it with "spirit light" and overlooked a rather important and obvious fact relating to this particular bird and one that I rather doubt the ancient Egyptians themselves would have overlooked. A little research would have informed them that, lo and behold, the crested ibis, as briefly mentioned earlier, is inextricably associated with the seasonal inundation of the Nile, because this particular bird was revered in ancient Egypt as the "harbinger of the inundation."

Here are just a few examples.

> People knew from long experience that this was about the time for the level of the Nile to start rising. Just before this, flocks of white ibises would have appeared on the fields as they returned from the south. If they came late or not at all, farmers would see this as a bad omen foreshadowing low floods and a poor harvest. So they regarded the wise bird that knew the secret of this vital phenomenon as an embodiment of the learned god Thoth.[6]

> In Ancient Egypt, sacred ibis were heralds of the flood, and symbolized the god Thoth, god of wisdom and master of time. They were also of practical use to the villagers, making pools safe to bathe by feeding on the water snails that carried the bilharzias liver parasite.[7]

> In Africa also we meet with the great Ibis (Tantalus ibis . . .), and the sacred ibis (I. religiosa), which is venerated in Egypt as the harbinger of the annual Inundation of the Nile, and was frequently embalmed and mummified.[8]

Given this rather unique quality of the ibis in "predicting" the imminent arrival of the annual Nile inundation, it is easy to understand how, in this sense, the ibis would be viewed by the ancient Egyptians as useful, beneficial, and illuminated. The Nile inundation was the lifeblood of the kingdom, and to have foreknowledge of its imminent arrival (or not) would have been most beneficial to ancient Egyptian farmers.

That conventional Egyptologists hold that the function of the early, giant pyramid was as an instrument of rebirth for the king is but an assumption that derives from their corresponding presumption that these pyramids were built as tombs for ancient Egyptian kings. If, however, we adopt the alternative view that the Giza pyramids (and all others of this period) were built not as instruments of rebirth for the king but rather as instruments of rebirth for the kingdom after the anticipated great deluge of Thoth (just as the Arab chronicles tell us), then in this sense Khufu's akhet (Khufu's "place of re-creation" or "place of reemergence") is equally valid, if not more so, given the use of the ibis hieroglyph and the bird's connection to Thoth and its wisdom as the harbinger or messenger of the coming deluge. And whereas the seasonal Nile flood (akhet) is symbolized by the use of the flooded land strip with plants sprouting forth, the great deluge or akhet spoken of by Thoth is symbolized by the ibis, the wise bird that was illuminated with the knowledge of Thoth and who knew of Thoth's coming deluge, the bird as the harbinger of the flood. And to reinforce this idea, we are presented with a determinative of the pyramid "emerging" from the flooded land.

So it seems to me that the term *akhet* has three different meanings, all of which have the same underlying concept—reemergence (rebirth) from water, to wit:

1. Akhet: when the sun is reborn by reemerging from the waters of the watery underworld to shine again on the eastern horizon (figure 5.2).
2. Akhet: when the crops are reborn by reemerging from the waters of the annual Nile inundation (figure 5.3).
3. Akhet: when the kingdom (i.e., the primeval mound of the Earth symbolized by the pyramid and flooded-land determinative) is reborn by reemerging from the great deluge of Thoth, just as it did in the First Time of creation (figure 5.4).

Akhet—when the sun, the crops, and the Earth are reborn or reemerge from water. And this idea may well explain the use of the hatched-disc glyph (*kh*), which some Egyptologists believe to be a placenta and is often colored red. Without the placenta, birth is not possible, and every human birth is preceded by waters; we are all born out of water.

So, whether it be depicted with the ibis or the land strip with growing plants or indeed as the later version of the sun disc between two mountains, the term *akhet* is to be related to rebirth or reemergence from water. Indeed, some versions of *akhet* with the sun disc between two mountains actually look more like the sun rising out of the sea, whereby the two "mountains" actually appear more like the crest of two waves with the sun rising from the trough in the middle—the sun emerging from the watery underworld.

In *The Ancient Egyptian Pyramid Texts,* James P. Allen noted this: "The Living One [the sun] became clean in the Akhet."[9]

As arks, the early, giant pyramids were the means by which the kingdom itself could be re-created or could reemerge from the floodwaters of Thoth. In short *akhet* might not so much equate to "horizon" or "spirit," as believed by conventional Egyptology, but actually to a "process of re-creation through a reemergence from water." It should not, however, be automatically assumed that this re-creation or reemergence of Khufu's akhet should be referring to the re-creation or reemergence of the king; it is equally possible, if not more so, that the re-creation or reemergence associated with the Great Pyramid in its name of Akhet Khufu is to be connected with the reemergence of the *kingdom* (the land) from a great deluge.

Akhet Khufu—the place of rebirth or re-creation of the kingdom. With this name applying to the entire space around the Giza pyramids it should be no surprise to find that an inscription on the Dream Stele that stands between the paws of the Sphinx tells us that Giza is "the Splendid Place of the First Time" (meaning "of creation")—the place of Sp Tpy (pronounced Zep Tepi). By the ancient Egyptians constructing their great pyramid arks, creation (after Thoth's deluge) might be assured again, and the pyramid arks, in mimicking the original primeval mound that arose from the primordial waters of creation and from which everything in existence came out of, would reenact this emergence from the flood waters that occurred at the First Time—the kingdom reborn a second time.

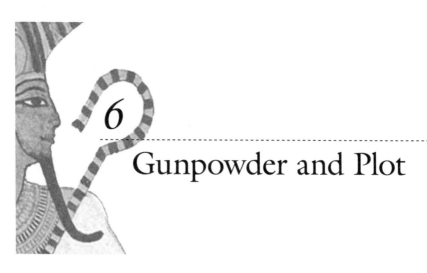

6

Gunpowder and Plot

Mr. Hill requested more gunpowder. . . . Two quarrymen were sent to blast over Wellington's Chamber.

COLONEL RICHARD WILLIAM HOWARD VYSE

This book would not be complete without comment upon a situation that is fast becoming a major source of embarrassment for conventional Egyptology. By including this chapter I hope to add my voice to the growing international demand that Egyptology conduct a thorough, independent scientific analysis of the inscriptions found within the Great Pyramid in 1837 by British adventurer and antiquarian Colonel Richard William Howard Vyse (figure 6.1). The need to reassess these inscriptions is all the more pressing given new evidence that has recently come to light concerning this discovery and the people involved in it.

The inscriptions are an issue that has been hotly debated for decades, if not longer. In 1837, Colonel Vyse, with the help of some "gunpowder archaeology," blasted his way into some hitherto-secret compartments above the King's Chamber of the Great Pyramid. Inside he found numerous painted "quarry markings" (graffiti), the

Figure 6.1. Colonel Richard William Howard Vyse

only writing ever discovered inside the monument. Among these unofficial quarry markings, Vyse and his team found a number of cartouches bearing the name of Khnum-Khuf, the full name of Khufu. In the topmost "Campbell's Chamber" they found the cartouche of Khufu—the king who, according to mainstream Egyptology, built the Great Pyramid circa 2550 BCE. They also discovered Khufu's "Horus name," *Mddw* (pronounced "Mededu" or "Medjedu"); in 1837 no one even knew that such a thing existed. These markings provided Egyptologists with the only tangible pieces of hard evidence directly connecting Khufu to the Great Pyramid and thus the Great Pyramid to the era of circa 2550 BCE.

Curiously though, the lowest of these chambers, discovered some seventy-two years earlier by Nathaniel Davison, was completely devoid of any such markings. This curious situation led some to speculate that perhaps Vyse's discovery was not so much a discovery at all but rather a fraud perpetrated by Vyse himself. However, Egyptologists reject such a notion based on two pieces of evidence.

1. No one in 1837 knew that the Horus name (the name the king took upon his ascension to the throne) existed let alone that Khufu's Horus name was *Mddw*.
2. There are quarry marks in tight gaps between the 70-ton granite blocks where no forger could ever hope to use a brush.

These two objections, however, can be easily dispelled. In the case of the Horus name we find that this was often written along with the king's birth name, that is, Khufu. First, if Vyse could recognize Khufu on a particular stone or document (and we shall see later in this chapter that he *could* recognize Khufu), then any other hieroglyphics that may have been written alongside—such as the Horus name—could also be copied. Vyse would know that whatever else was written—even although he couldn't read or understand it—was related to what he *could* read and understand—Khufu.

Second, with regards to placing painted marks in the tight gaps between the immovable granite blocks—this is not so difficult a task Egyptologists imagine it to be. (It should be said here, for clarity, that there are no cartouches in any of these tight spaces, just random mason's markings.) As independent researcher Dennis Payne informs us, by using a thin piece of wood, some string, and ochre paint a stencil could have been made. In this scenario the string forms the shapes of the relevant glyphs that are affixed onto a thin piece of wood and painted over with ochre paint. This thin wood with the painted marks is then inserted into the gap between the granite blocks. A thicker wooden board is then inserted behind the first board, jamming it against the granite block and thereby pressing the painted marks onto the block. When the wooden boards are removed we are left with the *illusion* of an impossible forgery—painted marks in a tight gap where no forger could ever use a brush. Thus Egyptology's two key objections to the forgery hypothesis are debunked.

But what about the actual paint? In 1837 red ochre paint (called *moghra*) was still being made according to the same ancient formula or recipe. Alas, however, at that time there was no scientific means to analyze the paint used to create the markings found in these hidden pyramid chambers, and so Egyptology had little option but to accept the authenticity of Vyse's discovery on simple trust, on his word.

QUESTIONS OVER VYSE'S CHARACTER

But was Vyse a man who could be trusted? Some thirty years earlier, in 1807, Vyse stood as a candidate in the Beverley constituency for the British Parliament. After Vyse won the seat (by a margin not seen before or since), Mr. Philip Staple (who finished a very poor third in the contest) presented a petition to Parliament, charging Vyse of electoral fraud.

> A petition of Philip Staple, Esquire, was read, setting forth, That at the late Election for Members to serve in Parliament for the Borough of Beverley, in the County of York, John Wharton, Esquire, Richard William Howard Vyse, Esquire, and the Petitioner, were candidates to represent the said Borough; and that the said John Wharton and Richard William Howard Vyse . . . each of them was guilty of bribery and corruption and corrupt practices in order to their being elected to serve as Members for the said Borough in the present Parliament.[1]

Unfortunately for Mr. Staple, his petition was not upheld. With the benefit of time, however, we now know it should have been, for it was discovered that of the 1,010 votes Vyse obtained in that election, 932 of them he secured with bribes. It has to be said, though, that in 1807 this was not an uncommon practice in rotten boroughs such as Beverley. But it also has to be said that not everyone who stood for Parliament was prepared to commit electoral fraud in order to secure victory. So, in this act, we have the first glimpse into Vyse's character; that he was a man who would do whatever it took, including perpetrating fraud, to achieve his goals.

Another charge of fraud leveled against Vyse is presented in his own published book, to wit:

> A slanderous paragraph, intended to be inserted in the English news-papers, was this day shown to me, which accused Colonel Campbell

of having improperly laid himself under obligations to the Pacha by obtaining the firmaun [a permit to excavate]; and which implied the Colonel and myself intended to make our fortunes under the pretence of scientific researches . . .[2]

Vyse makes no mention here as to the precise nature of the allegations being made against him. In what way did Colonel Patrick Campbell improperly obtain the firmaun (a permit, in this instance, for excavating in the Pyramids of Giza that had been issued in the name of Captain Giovanni Caviglia)? What was the extent of Vyse's involvement? How exactly were the two men planning to make fortunes "under the pretence of scientific research"? Who was behind these allegations, and what evidence did they have?

While Vyse's published work remains silent on these key questions, what this episode demonstrates is that someone believed that Vyse's activities in Egypt were improper, and this individual threatened, via the British press, to expose what Vyse was doing. Once again, Vyse's moral character is brought into question.

A DUBIOUS DISCOVERY

During his excavation at the third largest pyramid at Giza, the pyramid of Menkaure (G3), Vyse and his team found some human remains and a coffin lid bearing the name of Menkaure (in Greek, *Mycerinus*). On the surface this discovery appeared to have been the remains of an ancient Egyptian king in his pyramid tomb and, at that time, would have been the first king ever found (Howard Carter did not discover Tutankhamun's undisturbed shaft tomb in the Valley of the Kings until 1922). However, it was very quickly realized that the find was completely bogus. In this regard, renowned British Egyptologist Sir I. E. S. Edwards writes:

In the original burial chamber Col. Vyse had discovered some human bones and the lid of a wooden anthropoid coffin inscribed with the name of Mycerinus. This lid, which is now in the British Museum, cannot have been made in the time of Mycerinus, for it is of a pattern not used before the Saite Period. Radiocarbon tests have shown that the bones date from early Christian times.[3]

So, what we have here are archaeological artifacts from two quite different periods that are far removed from Menkaure's time and that have somehow magically found themselves together in Menkaure's pyramid, having been recovered by Vyse and his team only after other earlier explorers of this pyramid had somehow overlooked them. Why were the bones and coffin not of the same period? Are we to believe there were *two* intrusive burials from two different periods long after the time of Menkaure? Why, then, weren't any fragments of coffin or bones uncovered from the *other* intrusive burial (assuming, of course, that there were two such burials)? Do these events alone not reek of an attempt at deception by Vyse and/or his team, trying to pass off a "discovery" of an ancient Egyptian king that was later found to be false? If we have grounds here in Menkaure's pyramid to suspect attempted deception, we surely have to ask: Just how does this impinge upon the credibility of Vyse and his claimed discoveries elsewhere at Giza, including the inscriptions he allegedly discovered in the Great Pyramid?

A WITNESS TO DECEPTION

If all of this isn't bad enough for Vyse's reputation, then the 1954 handwritten family history of a Mr. Walter M. Allen of Pittsburgh, Pennsylvania, makes it a whole lot worse. It seems that Walter Allen's great-grandfather, Humphries Brewer, apparently worked with Vyse and his team at Giza in 1837 and witnessed Vyse's assistants, Mr. Raven and Mr. Hill, refreshing old paint and making new markings in the pyramid.

Humfrey [*sic*] received prize for bridge he designed in Vienna over Danube. H. Went to Egypt 1837. British Medical Serv. To Egypt. . . .

They were to build hospital in Cairo for Arabs with severe eye afflictions. Dr Naylor took Humfrey along. Treatment not successful, hospital not built. He joined a Col. Visse [*sic*] exploring Gizeh pyramids. Rechecked dimensions 2 pyramids. Had dispute with Raven and Hill about painted marks in pyramid. Faint marks were repainted, some were new. Did not find tomb. . . .

Had words with a Mr Hill and Visse when he left. He agreed with a Col. Colin [*sic*] Campbell and another Geno Cabilia [*sic*]. Humfrey went back to England late 1837.[4]

Curiously, while Vyse makes no mention of Humphries Brewer in his published book, he does refer to all the other individuals mentioned in Walter Allen's family account, including Dr. Naylor with his intention to help the local Arab people with severe eye problems. And as we can see from the Allen family record, it seems that his great-grandfather had a dispute with Vyse before leaving the site. Had Brewer objected to the marks being painted, perhaps accusing Vyse and his team of perpetrating a fraud, then it is hardly likely that a young man barely twenty years old and of little consequence to Vyse would have been mentioned in Vyse's finished work, his published account. That said, however, even though Vyse may not have mentioned Brewer by name in his book, he may have indicated his presence at the site through the work he would have done in the Great Pyramid. As Vyse notes:

Two quarry-men were sent to blast over Wellington's Chamber.[5]

This is precisely the kind of work in which Brewer, a civil engineer, would have been involved. One of these quarrymen, we know from Vyse's book, was a local Arab man named Daoud, but no mention is made therein of the name of the other—a man with expertise that would have been crucial to Vyse's ambitions. When he is so meticulous in naming everyone else in his book that was pivotal to his operations, why doesn't Vyse name the other quarryman?

While all of the above may leave a bad smell, an air of suspicion, it is not actual proof that Vyse perpetrated a fraud within the Great Pyramid. However, the most damning evidence of all comes from Vyse's own hand, and it shows beyond reasonable doubt that a deception *was* perpetrated by Vyse and his team within the Great Pyramid.

VYSE'S JOURNAL SPEAKS

In the absence of official scientific tests being done on these painted markings it seemed that the only avenue left to explore to try to determine their authenticity would be Vyse's *handwritten* journal from his time at Giza in 1837. I realized that if this document could be located then it might be possible to determine the accuracy of Walter Allen's account regarding his great-grandfather, Humphries Brewer. If Brewer had been in Egypt with Vyse in 1837, as Allen's account states, then it was perhaps possible that Vyse made mention of him in his handwritten journal (when they were on good terms) and simply redacted his presence from his published work after their dispute. That was my thinking, and if it turned out to be correct then it would at least offer some corroboration to Walter Allen's account.

And so, in March 2014, I set about looking for Vyse's handwritten journal. Thanks to the internet, it didn't take very long. I had searched for this document on the internet over the years and had always come up empty-handed, but this time the location of this nearly 180-year-old document came up: the Centre for Buckinghamshire Studies, in Aylesbury, England, about 400 miles from home. So my wife, Louise, and I would have to drive a round trip of 800 miles (1,288 km) to have a look at Vyse's journal. We didn't know what to expect or, indeed, if we would find anything at all of any great relevance to our quest. However, when we finally arrived at the center in early April 2014, we were not to be disappointed, though not in the way we had first imagined.

Vyse's handwritten journal consists of around 600 pages of yellowing, folded foolscap pages tied together in a bundle with a thin white ribbon and all contained within a rather unremarkable card folder. Although some of the pages are perfectly clear, the ink on many of the pages is exceedingly faint, browning with age. But this was the least of our problems with the document, as a quick glance of some of the pages would prove. Vyse's handwriting is almost impossible to read; a scrawling style where many letters are contracted or expanded and where a particular letter can take a different form depending on where it appears in a word. I had experienced doctors' prescriptions that were easier to read. In consideration of this difficulty, I sought permission to take digital photographs of the journal pages so that we could take them home to analyze at our leisure. Fortunately this wasn't a problem (as long as we didn't use flash photography). And so, for the next two days, Louise and I set about the not insignificant task of photographing each and every page of Vyse's handwritten journal plus some other material in his archive. It wasn't lost on us that the task to find anything significant from these pages could take months, if not years, to research thoroughly. (Indeed, a clear reference to the name Brewer has not, as yet, been found in Vyse's journal, although we have identified a few possible candidates that could very well be the name Brewer but that, at the time of writing, have not been confirmed by handwriting experts.)

It always seems to be the case, though, that just when your research seems to have hit the buffers, the "library angel" appears and hands to you exactly what you need, just when you need it—and so it turned out to be the case here. The gods of serendipity were on our side.

Hour after hour we had been turning and photographing the pages, seeing nothing before us but an endless, meaningless scrawl. As Louise turned one of the pages for me to photograph, I noticed that it had some hieroglyphics on it. Very few pages had such content, and so it was easy to catch the eye. But this wasn't just any old hieroglyphic markings that Vyse had written, it was the cartouche of Khufu, the king Egyptologists believe built the Great Pyramid.

Resting the camera on the table, I took a closer look at the cartouche

Vyse had drawn and pointed something out to Louise. We both then looked at each other in stunned silence as the realization and enormity of what we were seeing sank in—for before us was compelling evidence that the cartouche of Khufu, which Vyse claimed to have discovered within the Great Pyramid, must, in fact, have been forged by him—as a number of people over the years have long suspected. To say we were dumbstruck by what we had uncovered would be an understatement—evidence that proved, beyond reasonable doubt, that Vyse had perpetrated the hoax of all history.

After we returned to our hotel late that evening, not a little exhausted from our day's efforts, we sat and stared at our laptop screens in bemused silence at the evidence before us, struggling to wrap our minds around its game-changing implications. The irony of what we had found was not lost on us. Here we were, barely able to read a few words of Vyse's own handwriting and yet the ancient Egyptian script he had so carefully copied into his journal revealed to us the truth of the disputed inscriptions in the Great Pyramid that many have been seeking for decades, if not longer: they had been faked.

ANOMALIES IN THE CARTOUCHES

On the surface, the hieroglyphics within the two cartouches (the oval shapes) in figures 6.2a and 6.2b appear unremarkable. When we look at them a little closer, however, the simple truth they hold quickly becomes apparent.

The cartouche in figure 6.2a is a reproduction of the cartouche that we actually observe today in Campbell's Chamber of the Great Pyramid; the cartouche Vyse presents in his published book and which he claimed to have found in the monument. But in Vyse's handwritten journal another, slightly different, cartouche (figure 6.2b) is presented as having been found by him in Campbell's Chamber. Indeed, in his journal Vyse writes alongside this slightly different cartouche "in Campbell's chamber." However, a close examination of the cartouche

Image: Scott Creighton

Figure 6.2a. Reproduction of the Khufu cartouche as it appears (vertically) in Campbell's Chamber of the Great Pyramid. Note the disc has three small lines.

Image: Scott Creighton

Figure 6.2b. Reproduction of the Khufu cartouche allegedly from Campbell's Chamber as presented (horizontally) in Colonel Vyse's journal on June 16th, 1837. Note the disc does not contain any of the lines as noted in figure 6.2a—it is blank.

in Vyse's written journal shows a clear and highly significant difference between his journal entry and what is actually extant in the chamber, in particular, the small circle at the end (right-hand side) of the cartouche (figure 6.2b).

Whereas the vertical cartouche in the actual chamber (figure 6.2a) has a circle containing three lines (hatchings), the circle in the horizontal cartouche of Vyse's handwritten journal (figure 6.2b) presents only a *plain disc* with no center lines whatsoever. The question has to be asked—why would Vyse draw the cartouche differently in his journal from what we actually observe today in the chamber?

A number of possibilities to try to explain this anomaly have been proposed. Perhaps Vyse simply did not observe the lines in the disc in the chamber when he first made this entry in his journal on June 16th? However, this is unlikely for a number of reasons.

1. Vyse states quite categorically in his published book that Campbell's Chamber, in which the Khufu cartouche was found, was "minutely examined" for markings. If the chamber was "minutely examined," it seems unlikely that Vyse would have missed these markings in the disc.

2. Vyse manages to observe the two small dots under the snake glyph of the cartouche so one must presume that, having observed this small detail, he would have easily observed the much larger and more prominent lines in the disc glyph.

3. Vyse had already opened a number of other chambers before Campbell's Chamber and in those other chambers had found a total of six cartouches of Khnum-Khuf, *all* of which had a disc with center markings of some kind. As such, when Vyse finally opened Campbell's Chamber (the last chamber), he would surely have been fully anticipating finding the Khufu disc with similar center markings. Given his experience of the six marked discs found in the chambers below, finding no markings in the Khufu disc would most surely have piqued his curiosity and he would most certainly have double-checked it.

4. We observe elsewhere in Vyse's journal that he has drawn the cartouche of Khnum-Khuf with a similar-size disc on the page, complete with center markings (albeit quite faint markings).

5. This wasn't the only Khufu cartouche that Vyse drew in his journal without the three hatch lines. There were two such Khufu cartouches in his journal; one entry on May 27th and another on June 16th, 1837—both *without* the hatch lines. Furthermore, on May 30th, Vyse's assistant, Mr. Hill, was tasked by Vyse to make a facsimile copy of the Khufu cartouche

in Campbell's Chamber. Mr. Hill's drawing (which I viewed in the British Museum) contains the three lines in the disc and yet, on June 16th, more than two weeks after Hill's drawing had been completed, Vyse *again* enters the Khufu cartouche into his journal with just a plain disc. Why did Vyse make a mistake and then repeat the same mistake, even though Mr. Hill's facsimile would—presumably by this time—have shown him the three lines in the disc?

And yet, for all of this, in his written journal Vyse renders the Khufu cartouche from Campbell's Chamber without *any* of the hatch lines we see in that cartouche today. Perhaps, as some have suggested, Vyse was merely making a rough note of the cartouche in his journal? Again this proposal does not stack up for the following reasons.

1. Vyse was detailed and meticulous enough to draw the two small dots under the snake glyph (which are actually a mistake and not part of Khufu's name). If this was merely a rough drawing, why would Vyse be so precise with this small detail under the snake glyph and then be so casual with the more obvious detail within the disc?

2. Vyse would have been fully aware that he would be using his written journal (including the various drawings he made therein) as the basis from which to write his future book. Accuracy would have been of paramount importance to him and such detail would have been crucial to that accuracy—and especially so given that Vyse was in no way a specialist in this field. Neglecting to copy fairly obvious detail from the cartouche of a king could have caused serious interpretative consequences for scholars back in London, and Vyse would almost certainly have understood that. He wouldn't have a second chance at this—he had to get it noted correctly the first time.

So, we have to ask: Why did Vyse, against all normal and rational expectation, copy the cartouche from Campbell's Chamber into his journal and leave out the three lines from the cartouche disc? Why would he copy it down differently from what we actually see in the chamber today when detail and accuracy was paramount? And why would he copy it down this way *twice* in his journal when, surely, Mr. Hill's facsimile drawing should have alerted him to the proper spelling?

There is but one rather simple explanation to all of this. The crucial point to understand here is that *both* these spellings of the Khufu name are, in fact, *correct*. This is to say that, according to mainstream Egyptology, the name Khufu can be written with either a hatched disc *or* a plain disc, and numerous examples of both spellings exist in the archaeological record. However, in 1837 this fact wasn't yet fully understood, and this ambiguity in the spelling of Khufu is what resulted in Vyse having doubts and his subsequent deliberations. If he had sent a facsimile copy of the Khufu cartouche back to London with the wrong spelling, he would have been immediately discovered as a fraudster. If Vyse could be the first to empirically connect the Great Pyramid to Khufu then his name would be immortalized. He had to get it right.

Now, were it only the hatched-disc version of the Khufu disc that was extant in the historical record then the plain disc examples we find in Vyse's journal could simply have been explained away as an incomplete diary entry; a simple mistake or oversight. But given that the plain disc version of the Khufu cartouche *also* exists in the archaeological record leads us to an intriguing possibility: Did Vyse originally find an example of a Khufu cartouche with just the *plain* disc, which he copied into his journal (and presumably into the Great Pyramid), believing this version of the Khufu cartouche to be the correct and only spelling of the king's name? And did Vyse discover, some time later, that, in fact, there were examples of the Khufu cartouche with *hatched* discs, leading him to perhaps believe (wrongly) that the plain disc version he had originally found (and had placed in the Great Pyramid) had simply been an unfinished hatched disc (by the ancient Egyptian scribe who originally created it) and that to render the Khufu name fully and correctly required the plain disc to have hatched lines added? There is compelling evidence from Vyse's journal that this does seem to have been the case, as we will see shortly.

As can be seen in figure 6.3, in his entry from June 16th, Vyse has drawn *two* Khufu cartouches on the same page of his journal, *both* of which he states are from Campbell's Chamber and yet they have different discs in the cartouche.

However, because there is only *one* Khufu cartouche in Campbell's Chamber, they cannot both be right. And so it is that here, on this page of his written journal, lies the very essence of Vyse's doubt, contradiction, and his deliberation. Here on this page we observe Vyse contemplating a necessary change to what he once believed was the correct spelling of Khufu—the original plain disc version of the cartouche that he had written into his diary and had copied into the Great Pyramid actually required three lines to be added—or so he believed. Here on this page of Vyse's diary we find the evidence that lays bare the hoax of all history.

Why these deliberations at all—and why now? This controversial

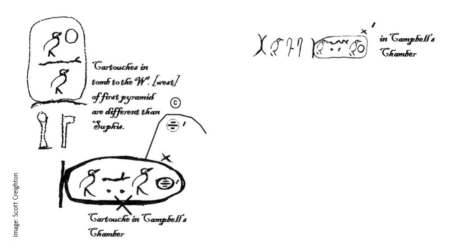

Figure 6.3. Reproduction of Vyse journal entry from June 16th, 1837. Note: there is more text on the original page of Vyse's journal than is shown in this reproduction.

diary entry had been made some three weeks *after* Vyse had opened and entered Campbell's Chamber—what was it that had occurred to make Vyse suddenly interested and start deliberating the spelling of this cartouche some three weeks after he had found it? A clue is given in the journal entry from June 16th (figure 6.3), when Vyse writes:

Cartouches [plural] in tomb to the W. [west] of the first pyramid are different than Suphis [Khufu].[6]

The above comment tells us two things.

1. Clearly from this comment Vyse already knew (or *believed* he knew) how the Khufu cartouche *should* be written and that he knew this long before the cartouche (i.e., Mr. Hill's facsimile drawing of it) had been sent to the experts in London for verification. This also implies that Vyse had a secret source of fairly accurate information.

2. Vyse had now realized some Khufu cartouches were spelled slightly differently (with hatched disc) and was interested in this spelling variation enough to make a visit to this tomb (the "Tomb of the Trades") to study this difference for himself.

But what had prompted Vyse to make this visit to this tomb to the west of the Great Pyramid in the first place? Why was he so interested in studying the Khufu cartouches there three weeks after its discovery in the Great Pyramid? Why was it now so important to him? Was it perhaps that he was up against a deadline? In just a few days time the cargo ship bound for London would be setting sail from the port at Alexandria, and Vyse wanted Mr. Hill's facsimile drawing of the Khufu cartouche aboard that ship, spelled correctly, of course. If so, then Vyse had to make sure the cartouche was correctly written before sending off Mr. Hill's facsimile to London, thus his late visit to the Tomb of the Trades is perhaps explained.

As noted above, in his journal Vyse writes that the Khufu cartouches in the tomb of the trades were "different than Suphis [Khufu]." However, on June 2nd (two weeks earlier) he had actually been sent drawings of the Khufu cartouches from this tomb by another of his assistants, Mr. Perring, showing two Khufu cartouches with hatched discs (figure 6.4). So Vyse had known for two weeks of the differently spelled Khufu cartouches in this tomb.

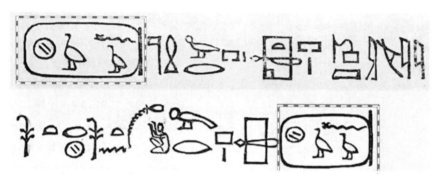

Figure 6.4. Khufu cartouches (with hatched disc) from the Tomb of the Trades. Image from Vyse, "Operations," Vol. II, 7–8.

Why did Vyse not simply accept Mr. Perring's drawings of these Khufu cartouches sent to him on June 2nd? Did Vyse perhaps think that Perring had made a mistake in his drawings thereby forcing Vyse to go to this tomb to verify these cartouches for himself? Whatever his motivation, Vyse now learns of the difference in spelling between the different Khufu cartouches and makes a note of this in his journal: "Cartouches in tomb to the W. [west] of first pyramid are different than Suphis." The Suphis/Khufu cartouche being referred to here would obviously be the cartouche that was in Campbell's Chamber at that time, with only the plain disc, just as he had drawn it in his journal. Logically then, were the cartouche in Campbell's Chamber to have contained a hatched disc at that time then Vyse would not have written that the cartouches in the Tomb of the Trades were *different* from Suphis/Khufu but that they were the *same*.

And so it is that this casual remark made by Vyse in his journal belies the truth of the situation—if the cartouches in this tomb contained hatched discs and were described by Vyse as "different," it implies, logically, that the disc of the Khufu cartouche in the Great Pyramid must, at this time, have been *blank*.

And so, having now observed and verified the spelling of the cartouches in the Tomb of the Trades for himself, armed with this new information, Vyse now acts—he sets about making the necessary changes. His deliberations over these changes can clearly be observed in his journal, as I will demonstrate step by step in figures 6.5–6.9 (see pages 126–27).

First Vyse would have drawn onto this June 16th entry of his journal the original Khufu cartouche (from his secret source) with just the plain disc. He writes alongside this: "cartouche in Campbell's" (for this is how he *originally* had it inscribed in the chamber; that is, with a blank disc). This is his *master copy*.

Next he creates an enlarged *working copy* of his master cartouche in the space at the bottom-left of the page—this will receive his revisions. At this point he copies the disc in the working copy *exactly* as it is in the master; that is, *without* any hatched lines. Underneath the working copy he writes: "Cartouche in Campbell's Chamber." So, at this point there is no contradiction between the two cartouches on the page as one is merely an enlarged working copy of the other (master), and, at this point in his deliberations, this *was* the cartouche in Campbell's Chamber, with just a plain disc.

But now, armed with his new information from the Tomb of the Trades, Vyse then places an "X" under his working copy (see figure 6.5 on p. 126) at the bottom of the page, marking it "wrong."

More specifically, however, Vyse then places a small "X" above each of the plain discs of the master and working copy of the cartouche—they are both "wrong" (see figure 6.6 on page 126).

Next Vyse draws another circle within the plain circle of his working copy cartouche and within this inner circle, he places three hatched lines (figure 6.7 on page 126).

Figure 6.5. Reproduction of Vyse's June 16, 1837, journal entry showing the working copy cartouche (with blank disc) crossed through with an X, indicating that it is "wrong."

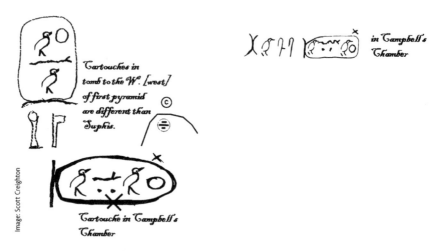

Figure 6.6. Reproduction of Vyse's June 16th, 1837, journal entry in which Vyse has placed an "X" ("wrong") above the plain discs of both cartouches on the page.

Figure 6.7. Reproduction of Vyse's June 16th, 1837, journal entry showing where Vyse inserts a hatched disc inside the plain disc of his working copy cartouche.

This is why, if we look closely at this page (figure 6.8), all other discs on the page are drawn with a *single* outline but the disc in the enlarged cartouche is drawn with a *double* outline—this hatched disc is essentially a composite image, a hatched disc on top of (or inserted into) what was once a plain disc—a disc within a disc.

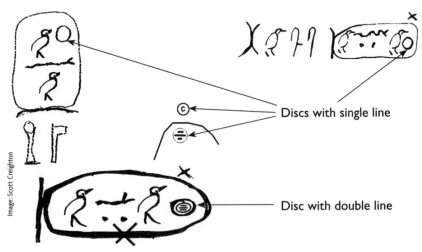

Discs with single line

ⓒ

Disc with double line

Image: Scott Creighton

Figure 6.8. Reproduction of Vyse's June 16, 1837, journal entry showing how all discs on the page are drawn with a single outline except the disc in the working copy cartouche (bottom left), which has a double outline. This is the result of the hatched disc inserted into the hitherto plain disc—a composite disc within a disc.

Finally, Vyse cross-references his change by placing a small vertical stroke above each of the two hatched discs (figure 6.9).

The revised cartouche is now ready to be placed in Campbell's Chamber; that is, three lines would now be added to the blank disc in the chamber cartouche (and, of course, a small update made also to Mr. Hill's facsimile drawing of the cartouche from May 30th before it is sent to London).

Having now made all the necessary changes and cross-references, Vyse neglects to remove the legacy and now redundant X marks on

Figure 6.9. The small hatched disc inserted on the page above the cartouche is cross-referenced with the hatched disc in the revised cartouche using a small vertical stroke.

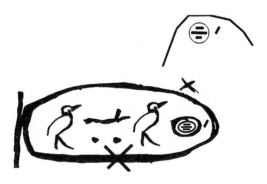

the journal page. He also neglects to remove or strike out the comment: "in Campbell's Chamber" from his master cartouche for this is no longer what is actually now in Campbell's Chamber—after Vyse's edit the original comment here now becomes a contradiction. But these are merely legacy marks and comments of a work in progress. No one except Vyse was ever meant to see this journal page and learn the truth of his last-minute edits, so there was little imperative for him to remove the contradictions this page of his journal now presents.

There is, however, something of an irony to all of this. Had Vyse simply kept the plain disc in the cartouche in Campbell's Chamber (instead of believing it was an unfinished hatched disc), his deception would actually have been far more convincing, because, as stated, Egyptology now knows that the plain disc *can* in fact render the name Khufu. But, as stated earlier in this chapter, no one in 1837 fully understood that; and so Vyse, in his ignorance, felt compelled to make absolutely certain of the name by adding the three lines into the disc. He overegged the pudding.

But who would actually place the markings in Campbell's Chamber and where would they be placed? Once again, Vyse's journal seems reasonably clear on the matter. In his May 27th entry—the day he first opened and inspected Campbell's Chamber—he writes:

> For Raven & Hill. These were my [?] marks from cartouche [image of cartouche with plain disc] to inscribe over any plain low [?] trussing.[7]

It is perhaps worth mentioning here that a trussing is a triangular support for holding up a structure. The triangular gabled roof of Campbell's Chamber supports the weight of the pyramid above and, in this regard, could be considered a "trussing." And it is a fact that the Khufu cartouche (and crew name) is to be found, painted vertically, on a low part of the gabled roof trussing.

It must be reiterated here, however, that Vyse's handwriting, for the most part, is sorely difficult to comprehend and that the above transcript from his journal is the result of many weeks of studying and analyzing that piece of text by myself, my wife, a number of family members, work colleagues, and close friends, as well as a couple of handwriting experts. While it was impossible for anyone to be absolutely certain that the transcription presented above is entirely accurate, most agreed that it is a fair and reasonable transcription of this particular passage from Vyse's journal. In fairness, though, and just to be perfectly clear, the difficulty in reading Vyse's handwriting obviously means that this transcription may not be perfectly accurate and will most likely require other handwriting experts to study the material to determine the matter conclusively.

If, however, this transcription does accurately reflect Vyse's May 27 journal entry (and, given the analysis of Vyse's June 16 journal entry, I personally have little reason to think otherwise), then what we have here is essentially an explicit instruction from Vyse to his assistants, Raven and Hill, to render a cartouche of Khufu (with plain disc) onto a low part of the gabled roof within Campbell's Chamber of the Great Pyramid—precisely where it is to be found today. As such this passage may well provide corroboration of Walter Allen's account of his great-grandfather, Humphries Brewer, who, in 1837, had argued with Raven and Hill about painting marks in the pyramid. Accepting that it has been transcribed accurately, this passage then represents incontrovertible proof that the Khufu cartouche in Campbell's Chamber of the Great Pyramid is a fake, placed there by Vyse and his team in 1837.

But the story does not end there. There is yet *more* evidence of this deception for consideration. As a consequence of the material uncovered in Vyse's journal, further questions arose concerning the facsimile drawings Vyse instructed to be made by his assistant, J. R. Hill, of the hieroglyphics allegedly found in these hidden chambers. What was found in Hill's facsimile drawings of the hieroglyphics in these hitherto hidden chambers was further evidence of the hoax.

THE LIE OF THE LANDSCAPES

This piece of evidence comes from something that is so obvious, no one ever actually notices it or, if they do, they think there is little relevance to it. It may seem something of a fastidious point, but the orientation of all three Khufu cartouches from Campbell's Chamber we find in Vyse's written journal are all oriented *horizontally*—but why should this be when the actual cartouche in Campbell's Chamber (figure 6.2a) is *vertically* oriented at 90° to Vyse's drawing of it (figure 6.2b)?

It may seem a trivial point, but when we consider Vyse's entire journal, we find that he has drawn other hieroglyphics exactly and correctly as he would have observed them in the various chambers; sometimes upright, sometimes upside-down (i.e., rotated 180°), and sometimes sideways (i.e., rotated 90°). With his body as the frame of reference (head to top of chamber, feet to bottom of chamber), this then presents us with evidence of how Vyse *instinctively* would draw the glyphs he observed in the chambers along with their specific orientation relative to the axis of his body—in short, he drew in his journal exactly what was in front of him, maintaining the appropriate orientation of the glyphs as he saw and drew them in his journal.

We surely have to ask then, given the *other* examples of glyphs in his journal, why then did Vyse decide to draw the three Khufu cartouches we find in his diary some 90° differently from how this cartouche actually appears in the chamber? In short, the Khufu cartouche is painted *vertically* on a gabled ceiling block of the chamber, so why didn't Vyse maintain its orientation (as he did with his other journal drawings) and draw the cartouche vertically in his journal rather than horizontally? Are we perhaps detecting here a clue as to how Vyse *originally* saw the Khufu cartouche and, therefore, why it takes this orientation in his written journal? Did Vyse originally copy a Khufu cartouche from some other place where the cartouche was *horizontally* aligned? Did Vyse simply copy what he had found in some other place into Campbell's Chamber (by Raven and Hill) and, without fully thinking through the ramifications of the next decision, had the original horizontal cartouche rotated by 90°, placing the glyphs vertically into the chamber thereby creating the contradiction with his horizontal journal entries?

Admittedly, this particular line of questioning may seem somewhat pedantic, but, remarkably, we find that it is a behavioral pattern that is emulated in the facsimile drawings of his assistant, J. R. Hill, and to a quite remarkable degree.

HILL'S ORIENTATIONS

During some unrelated research in 2013, I had been sent copies of three of Mr. Hill's facsimile drawings by Patricia Usick, Ph.D., of the British Museum. In studying these drawings I felt there was something odd about them, but, at the time, I couldn't quite put my finger on what it was I felt was wrong. I subsequently contacted Dr. Usick again in April 2014, asking if she could send me scanned copies of Mr. Hill's other facsimile drawings (twenty-eight in all) in order that I might be able to examine these to perhaps figure out what it was about them that was nagging in my mind. Unfortunately, Dr. Usick explained to me that there were no digital scans or photos of the other Hill facsimiles that she could send and that the only way I would be able to see them would be to arrange an appointment with her at the British Museum, which I duly did.

And so, on a beautiful spring day in May 2014, my wife, Louise, and I set off once again from our home in Glasgow, Scotland, for the British Museum in London (figure 6.10 on page 132). This time it would be a round trip of about 1,000 miles. We didn't know it then, but it was to be another trip filled with unexpected discovery.

After a couple of false starts searching the museum for Dr. Usick's department, we eventually met with her at the museum's information desk and she led us to the Egyptian and Near East Department's study room via some incredibly tortuous labyrinth through the museum. Indeed, from the information desk it took us a full ten minutes or so

Figure 6.10. The British Museum

to finally arrive at the study room, having passed through a number of long passageways, expansive hallways, and galleries, through a number of doors, up some stairs, through some other small rooms, down a service elevator, and finally into the room where Hill's drawings were at last presented to us. All around us there were numerous students and museum staff employed in analyzing and cataloging all manner of ancient artifacts. Dr. Usick took us to a table where Hill's facsimile drawings had already been laid out, awaiting our arrival. Once again we were permitted to photograph the material so long as we did not use flash photography.

The drawings had been placed in a very elaborate and robust folder whose dimensions were around two by three feet. A cream-colored panel on the front of the folder detailed the contents and was signed at the bottom "Colonel Howard Vyse" and below this, "1837." Fortunately, with only twenty-eight drawings to photograph this would be a much easier task for us than the 600 pages of Vyse's diary we had photographed the previous month. When, finally, we were able to view all twenty-eight of Hill's drawings, they told their own story and confirmed my suspicions about Vyse's horizontal diary entries of the Khufu cartouche—that the Khufu cartouche we find in his journal and in Campbell's Chamber had been copied by Vyse and his team from an original secret source that had been oriented *horizontally* when Vyse and Hill first copied it.

But how could we possibly determine this from only a brief study of Hill's drawings? The realization began to dawn when Louise picked up one of the facsimiles and was confused as to which way up it should be held in order for me to properly photograph it; that is, with the correct orientation of the hieroglyphics as they would have appeared to someone observing them in the chamber. The hieroglyphics on this particular drawing were oriented 90° to the signatures of the various witnesses, including Mr. Hill's signature (figure 6.11). I explained to Louise that many of the hieroglyphics in these chambers of the Great Pyramid were, in fact, painted upside-down or rotated at 90°. I further explained that Hill's signature, as well as the signatures of the other witnesses, essentially tell us the correct orientation of the hieroglyphics; the signatures should always be the right way up (like the north indicator on a map), which will then correctly align the hieroglyphics as they would appear to an observer in the chamber. And so we carried on, carefully photographing each of

Figure 6.11. Reproduction of the Hill facsimile showing hieroglyphics oriented 90° to Hill's signature (and other signatures on original). This is how the hieroglyphics would appear to an observer standing or crouching in the chamber. The facsimile hieroglyphics are given their correct orientation by the signature of Mr. Hill and the other signatories.

Image: Scott Creighton

J. R. Hill

Hill's facsimile drawings, ensuring the signatures (our compass) on the facsimiles were the right way up, thereby presenting to us the correct orientation of the hieroglyphics as they would appear in the chamber.

When we had finished our work and were checking the drawings on our laptops against the plan drawings by Mr. Perring of the hieroglyphics in the various chambers,* the penny dropped and I finally realized now what it was that had been nagging me for the best part of a year. The drawings Hill had made of the Khufu cartouche, which I had seen the year before, and crew name from Campbell's Chamber *both* had the wrong orientation relative to Hill's signature on the facsimile drawing.

This is to say that, almost without exception, Mr. Hill's drawings of the glyphs in the various chambers had the correct orientation relative to his own signature and the signatures of the other witnesses *except* the two drawings from Campbell's Chamber of the Khufu cartouche and crew name—the two facsimiles containing the very hieroglyphics I suspected Vyse had faked.†

Bizarrely, both of these facsimile drawings from Campbell's Chamber were signed by Mr. Hill (the *only* witness) as though he had been copying them from an original source that had the hieroglyphics oriented *horizontally* (figure 6.12), thereby providing corroboration that the cartouche and crew name facsimiles had come from some other place where the source had been presented with a different orientation (i.e., horizontal) to what we actually find in Campbell's Chamber (i.e., vertical). This then presents compelling evidence that Hill copied his facsimile drawing of the Khufu cartouche (and crew name) not from Campbell's Chamber but from somewhere else where it had been presented to him horizontally, hence why he unwittingly and habitually

---

*See Vyse, "Operations," Vol. 1, 279, 285.

†It should be noted here that we could crosscheck the orientations of only twenty-five of the twenty-eight facsimiles against Mr. Perring's plan drawing because Mr. Hill had drawn some glyphs that Mr. Perring had missed and vice versa, and thus the orientations could not be compared. Also, the orientations of some of Mr. Hill's drawings were compared against some fairly recent photos of the glyphs made by Colette Dowell and Robert Schoch, for which we were grateful.

J. R. Hill

Figure 6.12. Reproduction of the Khufu
Cartouche with Hill signature in landscape

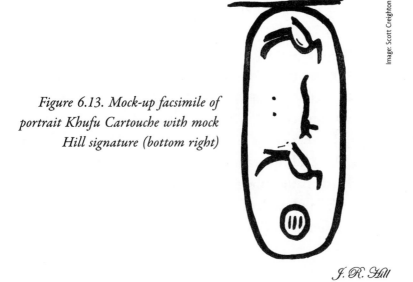

Figure 6.13. Mock-up facsimile of
portrait Khufu Cartouche with mock
Hill signature (bottom right)

J. R. Hill

signed the facsimile at the bottom (as most artists do), aligning his signature with the landscape orientation of the original.

If Hill had made this facsimile from the vertically aligned (portrait) hieroglyphics that we observe today in Campbell's Chamber (as is
believed), then, by following the normal convention he employed with
every other facsimile drawing he made that we were able to check, he
should have signed his Khufu facsimile as is shown in figure 6.13.

That Hill appears not to have followed his own convention in signing these facsimiles from Campbell's Chamber strongly suggests that these drawings had originally been copied from some alternative source where Hill *did,* in fact, follow his normal signing convention—he instinctively and habitually signed the drawing as he normally would at the foot of the horizontal/landscape drawing (figure 6.12), because that *was* the orientation of the *original* source cartouche. That Hill then, rather stupidly, decided to rotate his already signed landscape drawing 90° to copy it into the Great Pyramid was to be his undoing as it resulted in this very obvious discrepancy we find today. Had Mr. Hill simply copied this drawing into the chamber horizontally then his deception would have gone entirely unnoticed.

It seems somewhat ironic that Mr. Hill's signature placed on his facsimile drawings is used to vouch for the authenticity of the hieroglyphics in these chambers, and yet it is his signature that has, in the end, been his undoing, since, once again, the truth of these markings in Campbell's Chamber of the Great Pyramid is laid bare. And it has to be said—if Vyse and his team could change even just *three* markings in these chambers then their action taints *all* the markings found in Campbell's Chamber and all other chambers below; this evidence becomes the fruit of the poisonous tree.

A FINAL NOTE

In April 2013 two German researchers from Dresden University, Dominique Gorlitz, Ph.D., and Stefan Erdmann, accessed Campbell's Chamber of the Great Pyramid and while there removed (without any official permission to do so) a small sample of ochre paint from one of the hieroglyphs (not the Khufu cartouche), which they intended to have radiocarbon dated. At least one reporter, Dina Abdel-Alim of *Day 7 Magazine,* claims that the material had been radiocarbon tested by a German laboratory and that the paint was found to be only centuries old.*[8] Alas, when I contacted the German laboratory involved to ask them to confirm this report, they refused to confirm or deny anything.

WHERE NOW FOR EGYPTOLOGY?

With all of this evidence coming from a variety of sources, what we are presented with here is the smoking gun pointing to an incredible and quite audacious hoax having been perpetrated by Vyse and his team in the Great Pyramid in 1837.

It rather seems that wherever Vyse went and whatever field of human endeavor he operated, the whiff of scandal and of perpetrating some form of fraud was never too far behind. And so we now have to ask: Was Vyse a man whom we could truly say we can have complete confidence in? Can he be considered fully trustworthy, a reliable source? Is there anything in what we have learned that might raise sufficient doubt about this man that would lead us to question what he claims to have discovered in the Great Pyramid? In legal parlance what we have here is akin to asking is there reasonable suspicion—are there sufficient grounds to doubt the veracity of Vyse's published account as it relates to the discovery of these painted marks in the Great Pyramid? In short, is the discovery of these inscriptions Vyse's greatest achievement or his filthiest fraud?

If we take the view that there exist sufficient doubts on the character of Vyse and that there is now also sufficient evidence that casts doubt on his claimed discovery, how does this impact Egyptology and where then does Egyptology go from here? The answer is simple: Egyptology must do what it should have done in the first place with these inscriptions—consider them inadmissible evidence until proper science can verify their authenticity. Egyptology must put aside *all*

---

*It is quite possible to test ochre paint, because the binding agent used in ancient times would have been organic materials such as fish oil, honey, or gum.

written testimonies made concerning the markings in these chambers, including Vyse's published works, return to the actual, physical evidence itself, and apply hard science to try to determine the veracity of these inscriptions, for only then might the truth of these markings finally be settled.

It is not for myself or anyone else to *disprove* the authenticity of the inscriptions within these chambers—it is the responsibility of Egyptology to take these issues seriously and, if possible, to *scientifically prove* that these inscriptions *are* authentic, rather than dutifully trusting the word of a man whose actions have brought a number of others he crossed paths with in his life to question his moral rectitude. Egyptology's refusal to conduct official scientific research on these inscriptions in the face of mounting evidence that strongly suggests they were faked in 1837 is simply no longer a tenable position.

The world deserves to know the truth of these inscriptions.

7

Ages of Deluge
and Drought

After the usual interval, the stream from heaven, like a
pestilence, comes pouring down.

PLATO, *TIMAEUS*

When the ancient Egyptians measured the height of the stars and observed that they had departed from their normal course (i.e., the Earth's rotational axis had somehow become disturbed, giving to an Earth-based observer the apparent view that the stars had changed their positions), they believed that this change in the heavens would, some three hundred years in their future, result in a great deluge followed by a disastrous drought—flood and fire. And by constructing their great pyramid arks they hoped that, after the worst effects of this devastating catastrophe had passed, they would have the means to "reboot" their civilization.

The first thing to say here is that, whether the anticipated deluge and drought actually came to pass is actually a secondary issue. The key consideration here is that, in observing the changed heavens, the ancient

Egyptians *believed* the change would result in these catastrophes, and the mere belief that these disasters were certain to occur in the not-so-distant future was motivation enough for them to put in place the necessary countermeasures (i.e., the construction of their giant pyramid arks to help guard against such a devastating outcome). But was such a belief justified? Was the need for the construction of their great pyramid arks vindicated? What evidence is there to support that such catastrophes—deluge and drought—actually came to pass?

DELUGE

The history (and prehistory) of humanity is a litany of ancient flood stories. From all over the world and from just about every known culture, stories of destructive floods have come down to us, some that were said to have been so devastating that only a few people survived to repopulate the Earth. Those of a religious faith will point to the truth of a single, worldwide flood that is testified in various religious texts. Those of a more secular and scientific outlook will insist that such flood legends refer only to localized flooding events (from these various cultures around the world) rather than a single, devastating global deluge that many of a religious outlook believe took place and was divinely ordained in order to "cleanse" the Earth.

But what does science have to say on the subject? What evidence is there to support the idea of a single, devastating worldwide flood? In terms of our modern view of the world, the evidence of such a single global flood is probably best described as ambiguous; it rather depends on how the question is framed. Science tells us, for instance, that around twelve thousand years ago sea levels all over the world were around three hundred feet lower than they are today. Most of the world's population today lives on coastal areas, and there is little reason why this would not have been the same for populations thousands of years ago when sea levels were much lower. As such those coastal settlements and their populations all over the world would, over time, have been gradually inundated by the rising sea, forcing them to relocate to higher ground. Technically, this long, gradual rise in global sea levels could be described as a global flood, but this was not, in the main, the kind of apocalyptic sudden deluge that many ancient flood stories relate. These cataclysmic flood stories tell us that the deluge was rapid and overwhelming, indicating that sea levels rose very rapidly by a considerable amount all over the world and that this great deluge was somehow related to events observed in the heavens. Consider these examples, first from China and then from South America.

> Hereupon Nu Kua melted stones of the five colors to repair the heavens, and cut off the feet of the tortoise to set upright the four extremities of the earth. Gathering the ashes of reeds she stopped the flooding waters and thus rescued the land of Chi.[1]

> The pillars of heaven were broken. The earth shook to its foundations. The sky sank lower towards the north. The sun moon and stars changed their motions. The earth fell to pieces and the waters in its bosom uprushed with violence and overflowed . . . the system of the universe was totally disordered.[2]

How is such a sudden and overwhelming flood possible, and what evidence is there to support such rapid, devastating rises in global sea levels?

J. Harlen Bretz and Catastrophism

In the early twentieth century it was the established view of scientists that changes to the Earth's natural landscape occurred imperceptibly and slowly over very long periods of time. The idea that sudden massive flooding (catastrophism) could play a part in the molding and shaping of our planet was largely ridiculed by geologists at this time. But when J. Harlen Bretz, a geologist with the U.S. Geological Survey, made a visit to the Columbia Basin region in eastern Washington state, he discovered something in the peculiar landscape of this area that would challenge and ultimately change the long-held preconceptions of his peers.

Bretz published a paper in 1923, arguing that the channeled scablands in Eastern Washington State were caused by massive flooding in the distant past. This view, which was seen as arguing for a catastrophic explanation of the geology, was against the prevailing view of uniformitarianism, and Bretz's views were initially discredited. However, as the nature of the Ice Age was better understood, Bretz's original research was vindicated, and by the 1950s his insights were also vindicated.[3]

Bretz recognized peculiar features of the landscape in this area as unmistakable signs of catastrophic, massive flooding in the distant past (figure 7.1). Whereas the conventional view held that the erosion in

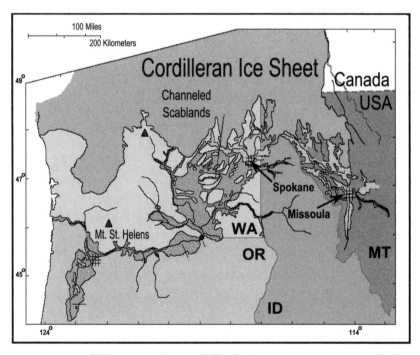

Figure 7.1. Cordilleran Ice Sheet and flood plains, circa 20,000 BP (before present). Image by United States Geological Survey.

this area occurred gradually over many tens of thousands of years as part of the planet's natural sedimentation and erosive processes, Bretz's view was that the landscape he observed had in fact been shaped almost instantly by a series of brief, cataclysmic megafloods.

As deglaciation accelerated and the great ice sheets retreated, meltwater would have formed great proglacial lakes, dammed up with a wall of ice or moraine. As the water pressure in the lakes increased from the melting ice, eventually the ice dams or moraines would have yielded to this pressure and collapsed, allowing a cataclysmic outburst of water to surge over the land, gouging and reforming it instantly. A number of these sudden 'megafloods' are now known to have occurred during the Holocene period. The last of these, from glacial Lake Agassiz, is believed to have occurred around 8,200 years ago. An article from the journal *Earth and Planetary Science Letters* discusses "a sea-level jump that occurred within the 8.18 to 8.31 ka time window and is attributed to the final drainage of proglacial Lake Agassiz–Ojibway. . . . The total inferred eustatic sea-level rise associated with the very final stage of LAO drainage at 8.2 ka ranges from 0.8 to 2.2 m, considerably higher than previous estimates."[4]

If this final, massive outburst of glacial Lake Agassiz rapidly increased sea levels all over the globe by the upper estimated limit of 2.2 meters (7.2 feet), this would have had catastrophic effects for the people in just about every coastal settlement on the planet, giving no time for them to adapt and relocate; they would have simply been swept away. And the memory of such a catastrophic deluge would surely have been written into legend by cultures all over the world.

So, while it is true that sea levels at the end of the last ice age generally increased slowly (by some three hundred feet) throughout the Holocene period, causing relatively little difficulty for global populations to adapt, this gradual rise was occasionally punctuated by dramatic leaps as a result of the sudden collapse of glacial dams and the massive outbursts of freshwater from the great proglacial lakes into the Earth's oceans. Such sudden and dramatic increases would have given many of the Earth's coastal settlements little chance.

But it seems that even the gradual, upward rise in global sea levels seems to have occurred much quicker than scientists have hitherto realized. The discovery of ancient mangrove forests under the Great Barrier Reef gives an indication of just how quickly the general rise of global sea levels actually was.

> The discovery of ancient mangrove forest remains under the Great Barrier Reef has cast doubt on some theories about how quickly the sea level rose after the last ice age.
>
> Most scientists believe it was a gradual rise over the past 9,000 years. But the existence of relic mangroves 70cm (27in) below the floor of the Barrier Reef, some with leaves and branches still intact, suggests an abrupt rise.
>
> Dan Alongi, a biologist at the Australian Institute of Marine Science, said it appeared that sea levels rose about 3 meters in less than 30 years, drowning forests and flooding estuaries, 20 times faster than previously thought.
>
> "Material was very much intact, it didn't even have time to fully decompose when it was buried," he said. "So it does tell us that when climate change last happened it was comparatively quick."
>
> It could indicate how quickly the climate might change in future, he said, adding that a sudden rise in sea level of the same magnitude would cause widespread damage to coastal areas.[5]

DROUGHT

The aridification of Egypt was a process that had been occurring for many thousands of years, and the people were well used to dealing with such a dry climate, blessed as it was with the annual inundation of the Nile, which allowed the country to flourish. But this general aridification was also punctuated by droughts so severe that the country was brought to its knees, which, indeed, is believed to be one of the key contributing factors for the demise of the Old Kingdom. Proof of such devastating droughts is now being found in Lake Tana in Ethiopia, the source of the Blue Nile.

Two drought episodes occurred at 8.4 and 7.5 cal kyr BP [calibrated thousand years before present], and are also interpreted as a southward shift in the monsoon front. The first of these events appears to have preceded and been more significant than the 8.2 cal kyr BP. Precipitation declined after 6.8 cal kyr BP, although we do not see an abrupt end to the African Humid Period. This period culminated in a dry episode at ~ 4.2 cal kyr BP, supporting the view that reduced Nile flow was a contributing factor to the demise of the Egyptian Old Kingdom.[6]

Further research into this ancient drought that perhaps brought about the collapse of the Egyptian Old Kingdom was conducted by the University of St. Andrews.

Researchers from the University of St Andrews have confirmed that a severe period of drought around 4,200 years ago may have contributed to the demise of the [Egyptian Old Kingdom] civilization. Using seismic investigations with sound waves, along with carbon dating of a 100-metre section of sediment from the bed of Lake Tana in Ethiopia, the team were able to look back many thousands of years. They were able to see how water levels in the lake had varied over the past 17,000 years, with the sediment signaling lush periods but also times of drought.

Lake Tana—the source of the Blue Nile river—flows to the White Nile at Khartoum and eventually to the Nile Delta. Dr Richard Bates, senior lecturer in earth sciences at St Andrews, said their studies had confirmed that the ancient civilization that was the Egyptian Old Kingdom—often referred to as the Age of the Pyramids—may have experienced a prolonged period of drought of the same severity being seen in parts of Africa now.

"Part of this research was driven by whether we could see anything in the lake sediment that would help us understand more about that period of drought, which was during the 90-year period at the end of the Old Kingdom, which really caused its demise," he said. "There were great riots, and anarchy breaking out as a result of it."

Historical records have suggested the region was hit by a drought spanning several decades, forcing people to extreme measures with some writings even suggesting people were forced to eat their own children. This drought has now been confirmed by information collected by the St Andrews team, along with colleagues from the University of Aberystwyth.

Dr Bates said: "It was coming to the end of a particularly long period in the pharaohs and there is quite a good record that law and order was breaking down. Most of that comes as a result of pressures outside and in this case it was the failing agricultural system where that was such a dominant part of society, and the result of that being anarchy."

But Dr Bates said they had found evidence of much more severe droughts up to 19,000 years ago in Africa. "Those were way more severe than either the ones we have got today or this time period 4,200 years ago," he said. "That was significant, but actually within the last 100,000 years it was by no means the worst. That's interesting . . . we are getting droughts in different places that are causing severe conditions, but these are compared to the absolute worst ones that could and have happened, and by the law of succession will happen again."[7]

It appears then that around three hundred years after the construction of the pyramids had begun (according to conventional chronology), the Old Kingdom of ancient Egypt did (as anticipated by the builders of the early, giant pyramids) collapse and come to a relatively sudden and dramatic end as a result of an unprecedented drought.

This collapse of the kingdom would be followed by a period of chaos in ancient Egypt that would last for around two hundred years—the First Intermediate Period—after which ancient Egypt, unlike many other civilizations and cultures of the Near East that had also collapsed around that time, through the use of its great pyramid arks, would be able to reconstitute itself and rebuild its civilization from the ashes of its destruction.

But was this severe drought that seemingly ended the Old Kingdom actually the result of what the ancient Egyptians had witnessed in the stars some three hundred years or so previous, or was it merely a coincidence that the kingdom collapsed around the anticipated time? We may never know the truth of this. What can be pointed to, however, is evidence that indicates a storage-and-recovery function for the pyramids, evidence that suggests the ancient Egyptians of this period believed a major catastrophe was looming and had planned for it by building and storing all manner of "recovery goods" (including vast quantities of seed) in their great pyramid arks. In the pyramid complex of Djoser at Saqqara, for example, massive quantities of various seed types were stored under and around the vast complex along with some forty thousand storage-and-distribution vessels. Indeed, when the first explorers entered some of the underground galleries of this pyramid in the early twentieth century, they had to wade ankle-deep through vast quantities of grain. Consider the following examples.

> Archaeologists found a row of [simulated] granaries along the west half of the northern enclosure wall of Djoser's complex (3d dyn.), still filled ankle-deep with a mix of decayed grain, intact grains and even ears. Interestingly, the seals (from the decayed sacks) mention Djoser but also his predecessor Khasekhemui. Large stone vessels with the name of Khasekhemui were also found underneath the southern Mastaba, which has the shape of a granary. There were very few objects with Khasekhemui's name elsewhere in the complex.[8]

Once again, the investigation of the west mounds is not yet complete, but excavations here have shown that there are no chambers in their superstructures . . . five shafts and staircases provided access to the substructure, which is composed of long, partly destroyed corridors and projecting side chambers. In some sections, a large number of fragments of stone vessels were found, together with grains (barley and wheat) and dried fruit.[9]

Various complementary explorations in the Zoser complex were undertaken by Firth. He found in the northern area near a vast rock-cut altar, simulated store-rooms [granaries] above subterranean galleries containing great quantities of provisions of wheat, barley, sycamore figs and grapes.[10]

Finally, in the obviously unfinished northern part of the complex, there is a gigantic altar carved into the rock, with the remains of a limestone casing. Offerings must have been exposed on the altar before being taken, through a shaft 60m away, down into the storerooms that branch from a gallery running east-west. These chambers contained mostly wheat and barley.[11]

At the north end of the pyramid complex is a very large courtyard, still not fully cleared of debris, with an altar near the northern wall. Underground galleries along this wall contained real food—granaries of wheat and barley, but also figs, grapes, and bread. An extensive system of underground galleries, mostly inaccessible, is also located to the west of the pyramid and southern court. . . . Entered from 11 vertical shafts, some of the subterranean corridors lead to long narrow storerooms for an astonishing number of carved stone vessels (about 40,000!), many of which were made in the first two dynasties.[12]

EXPLOSIVE EVIDENCE

And there may be some further evidence to indicate that the primary purpose of the early, giant pyramids was to function as arks or recovery vaults to store massive quantities of grain and other seed types (along with other useful recovery items), and this additional evidence comes from a rather unusual and unlikely source—cracks within the walls and ceiling of the so-called King's Chamber of the Great Pyramid. These cracks were first noted by Sir William Matthew Flinders Petrie, who wrote:

> The crack across the Eastern roof-beam has been also daubed with cement, looking, therefore, as if it had cracked before the chamber was finished. . . .
>
> On every side the joints of the stones have separated, and the whole chamber is shaken larger. . . . At the S.W. corner, plaster is freely spread over the granite, covering about a square foot altogether. . . .
>
> These openings or cracks are but the milder signs of the great injury that the whole chamber has sustained, probably by an earthquake, when every roof beam was broken across near the South side; and since which the whole of the granite ceiling (weighing some 400 tons), is upheld solely by sticking and thrusting. Not only has this wreck overtaken the chamber itself, but in every one of the spaces above it are the massive roof-beams either cracked across or torn out of the wall, more or less, at the South side; and the great Eastern and Western walls of limestone, between, and independent of which, the whole of these construction chambers are built, have sunk bodily. All these motions are yet but small—only a matter of an inch or two—but enough to wreck the theoretical strength and stability of these chambers, and to make their downfall a mere question of time and earthquakes.[13]

As Petrie explains, the most popular explanation for these cracks is that they were possibly the result of an earthquake that shook the entire structure. This would imply, however, that earthquakes were highly selective in inflicting damage only to the King's Chamber of the Great Pyramid and somehow conspired to spare all other chambers and all other earlier pyramids from similar damage. Other commentators have suggested that the damage may have been caused by the explosive gunpowder charges set by Vyse almost directly above the King's Chamber in order to obtain access to the hidden relieving chambers (see chapter 6). But, as Petrie points out, the cracks in the King's Chamber had been filled with ancient plaster, thereby proving that this damage existed long *before* the destructive nature of Vyse's gunpowder archaeology.

So what *could* have damaged this chamber so much so that Petrie describes it as a "great injury" that finds "on every side the joints of the stones have separated, and the whole chamber is shaken larger"? From Petrie's description it almost seems as though there had been some almighty explosion within this chamber, but if such were the case then this begs the obvious question: What substance existed in ancient times that could possibly have caused an explosion so violent as to inflict such extensive damage?

A possible clue to the source for such a violent explosion was actually discovered by none other than Vyse—soot. In 1837 the British antiquarian wrote in his journal the following:

Upon first entering the apartment, a black sediment was found, of the consistence of a hoar-frost, equally distributed over the floor, so that footsteps could be distinctly seen impressed on it, and it had accumulated to some depth in the interstices of the blocks. Some of the sediment, which was sent to the French establishment near Cairo, was said to contain igneous particles. When analyzed in England, it was supposed to consist of the exuviae of insects; but as the deposition was equally diffused over the floor, and extremely like the substance on the 25th instant at the second pyramid, it was most probably composed of particles of decayed stone. If it had been the remains of rotten wood, or of a quantity of insects that had penetrated through the masonry, it would scarcely have been so equally distributed; and, if caused by the latter, it is difficult to imagine why some of them should not have been found alive when the place was opened evidently for the first time since the pyramid was built.[14]

It seems that, even today, there remain questions as to what this "equally distributed . . . black sediment" actually was. But given the premise as presented in this book that these early, giant pyramids were constructed as arks for the storage of various recovery items such as large quantities of various seed types, including (but not limited to) wheat and barley grain, how then is it possible that such relatively inert organic material could cause such a violent explosion within the King's Chamber? It just didn't seem possible.

Or so I thought until I had a chance discussion with John Ferguson, a fire consultant in my hometown of Glasgow, who informed me that large densities of grain dust contained within a confined space can, when ignited, result in tremendously powerful explosions. Researching this possibility further, I came across the following:

Scientist Explains Likely Cause of Grain Elevator Explosions

When grain dust mixes with oxygen and it meets fire, the results are explosive.

"It's very similar to a bomb," says Robert Henry, a science instructor at Wichita State University. "Basically, it ignites just like gun powder would."

In a demonstration, he filled the bottom of a straw with grain dust and blew it into an open flame a few inches away. It resulted in a fireball. He says this is identical to what could happen inside a poorly ventilated grain elevator when there's a spark.

"Most of the material that you see in a grain elevator is inert, it's packed. But in the process of milling the grain and transporting it around on belts and so on and so forth, you get these tiny particles that begin to float in the air. That's when it becomes dangerous."

He says the explosion is by a physical reaction as opposed to a chemical one.

"When you get a little bit of it and you disperse it in the air, there's a tremendous amount of surface area and that surface area being exposed to oxygen makes it extremely flammable."[15]

Ferguson further advised that postexplosion the burned grain dust would settle as a black, charcoal-like sediment. It is entirely possible, therefore, that the black, charcoal-like sediment found by the early explorers of these upper chambers of the Great Pyramid may in fact have found the burned remains of grain dust from a massive grain dust explosion within the Great Pyramid. If this is so then it seems that while the chambers within the Great Pyramid ark were either being filled (or emptied) with grain, a buildup of grain dust in the Grand Gallery occurred and that this was accidentally ignited, causing a primary explosion in the Grand Gallery, resulting in a much greater secondary explosion occurring in the confined space of the King's Chamber, causing the considerable damage to that chamber that we observe today. Black, burned grain dust would then have permeated and settled throughout the structure, and this may well have been the sediment found by Vyse and his team.

A GREATER ANTIQUITY

So, while there would appear to be considerable physical evidence that a severe drought contributed significantly to the collapse of the Old Kingdom (and other Near East cultures), the earliest scientific evidence of a major global flood having occurred—the final outburst of Lake Agassiz—took place circa 6200 BCE, thus, it would seem, long before the conventional construction date of the early, giant pyramids.

However, as mentioned previously, what the ancient Egyptians *believed* would happen in their future and what *actually* happened are two quite different issues. The key point here is that the ancient Egyptians *believed* a great deluge was imminent and that it would destroy their kingdom, and, as a result of that *belief,* they chose to take affirmative action; they built their great pyramid arks.

But there is yet another possibility to consider here, and, although somewhat controversial, it might also help explain the ancient Egyptian belief of a great deluge followed by drought. Perhaps what is needed is a quite different perspective; perhaps, as many alternative thinkers (myself included) have long suggested and suspected, the pyramids (and Sphinx) are of much greater antiquity than conventional Egyptology presently considers.

In my previous book, *The Giza Prophecy* (with coauthor Gary Osborn), evidence was presented that seemed to suggest a far greater age for the pyramids at Giza. This evidence took the form of an ostrich eggshell that archaeologists have dated to circa 4400 BCE (figure 7.2).

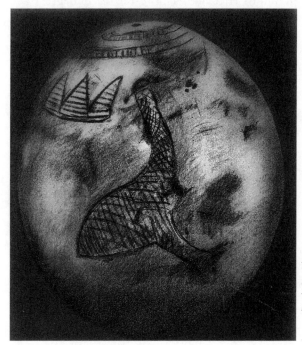

Figure 7.2. Ostrich egg depicting Giza pyramids (ca. 4400 BCE)

Image rendition by Gary Osborn

This eggshell seems to depict a rough map of the Nile Valley, including the Fayoum region and the Giza pyramids to the northwest.

If this eggshell truly is depicting the Giza pyramids, then it thoroughly contradicts the conventional chronology associated with these structures and demonstrates a much greater antiquity for them. This is to say that the Giza pyramids (and probably all of the early, giant pyramids) existed by *at least* 4400 BCE—but could be much older still.

Egyptologists, naturally, will point to the radiocarbon dating studies that have been carried out on the early, giant pyramids and claim that these prove the circa 2500 BCE provenance of these structures.

If only matters were that simple.

For a start there are many scientists who reject the science of radiocarbon dating as being seriously flawed. And second, even if radiocarbon dating *could* be relied on to deliver accurate dates for artifacts, all of the tests on the early, giant pyramids were taken from charcoal fragments caught in the mortar used to bind the pyramid blocks. Who is to say that the builders circa 2500 BCE were not actually *repairing* the pyramids that had, as a result of their great age, fallen into disrepair? And if we actually look around Giza and elsewhere, we find some compelling evidence to support the hypothesis that such reparation works appear to have taken place.

PYRAMID REPAIRS

Let us consider first of all the construction of the pyramid at Meidum, which was supposedly originally built as a step pyramid by Sneferu, who then, apparently, much later in his life, decided to convert this structure into a true pyramid with smooth sides. But what if we take a slightly different view here: What if the original builder of the Meidum step pyramid *wasn't* Sneferu at all but was perhaps some otherwise unknown builder from a much earlier time and Sneferu merely attempted to *convert* the original step pyramid structure he had "found" into a true pyramid? Certainly this would help explain Sneferu's apparent loss in pyramid construction prowess since, while the footprint of the step pyramid superstructure at Meidum was founded on a bed of solid rock, Sneferu attempted to apply his conversion of that pyramid (into a true pyramid) on a foundation of sand, hence, that is why the outer "true pyramid skin" added by Sneferu collapsed shortly after its completion (if it was ever completed at all).

And we have to ask: Why would Sneferu seem to understand that a massive stone structure like the Meidum step pyramid would only be structurally sound by building it on solid bedrock and then suddenly forget that basic engineering fact when he later tried to construct its conversion to a true pyramid on a foundation of sand? It rather seems to me that what these construction contradictions of the Meidum pyramid probably represent are two quite distinct building phases by two quite different builders—the first by someone who obviously understood basic engineering principles of solid foundations, and the second by someone who clearly did not (i.e., Sneferu building on sand). That both construction phases have been conflated by Egyptologists to be the work of one man simply makes little sense of the actual facts.

Everywhere at Giza and elsewhere we seem to be confronted by artifacts that seem to give the impression of being of a much earlier age and subsequently reshaped and/or reworked by later peoples. Take, for example, the casing stones of G3, the pyramid Egyptologists attribute to Menkaure. Unusually, the lower sixteen courses of casing stones were crafted from granite, while the upper layers had, according to conventional thought, all been crafted of white Tura limestone in accordance with all other pyramids (see figure 7.3 on page 156). Also noticeable is that G3's granite casing stones were not finished by smoothing and polishing them.

The original gleaming white limestone casing stones that once may have covered this entire pyramid (including the lower sixteen courses) were perhaps damaged or had otherwise fallen into disrepair, or were perhaps even stolen, and Menkaure perhaps was simply engaged in making reparations to the missing white casing stones with

Figure 7.3. Unfinished granite casing of G3

granite replacements—a stone that was much heavier and more difficult to work with and thus would be much more difficult to dislodge
or to steal.

There is, of course, also the possibility (as observed with the pyramid at Meidum) that all of the early, giant pyramids may originally have
been built as step pyramid structures and that the later Egyptians circa
2500 BCE simply attempted to convert *all* of them to true, smooth-
sided pyramid structures.

In this regard the passageways of Menkaure's Mortuary Temple are
also worth mentioning for it seems that here too much remodeling work
by Menkaure of a much older structure seems to have occurred, with
original limestone walls severely eroded with age having been refash-
ioned and contoured to receive a patchwork veneer of protective granite
blocks that have the appearance themselves of having been worked and
recycled from some other site. This type of "granite veneer" also appears
in the Sphinx Temple, as noted by Graham Hancock.

> Another point I noticed was that the Temple walls appeared to
> have been constructed in two stages. The first stage, most of which
> was intact (though deeply eroded), consisted of the strong and
> heavy core of 200-ton limestone blocks. On to both sides of these
> had been grafted a facade of dressed granite which (as we shall see)
> was largely intact in the interior of the building but had mainly
> fallen away on the outside. A closer look at some of the remaining
> exterior facing blocks where they had become detached from the
> core revealed a curious fact. When they had been placed here in
> antiquity the backs of these blocks had been cut to fit into and
> around the deep coves and scallops of existing weathering patterns
> on the limestone core. The presence of those patterns seemed to
> imply that the core blocks must have stood here, exposed to the
> elements, for an immense span of time before they had been faced
> with granite.[16]

It seems then that the more we look into the physical construction properties of these monuments, the more we are confronted with contradictory evidence, evidence that seems to point toward multiple construction phases and/or remodeling of already ancient structures by later cultures.

Foremost in these dating controversies of the Giza monuments is, of course, the Sphinx. The rebel Egyptologist scholar and writer John Anthony West, supported by Boston University Professor of Geology Robert M. Schoch, Ph.D., proposed for the Sphinx (based on the extensive erosion of the monument) a date thousands of years greater than that presently considered by mainstream thought. To date, this controversy has never been satisfactorily resolved; the jury is still out.

But the most remarkable aspect of this entire question as to the age of these structures is the fact that the ancient Egyptians themselves, in a text known as the Inventory Stele, actually wrote about the repairs they made to some of the monuments at Giza that were apparently already ancient. In this controversial text we are told the following:

Long live the Mezer, the King of Upper and Lower Egypt, Khufu, given life. He made for his Mother, Isis, the Divine Mother, Mistress of the Western Mountain, a decree made on a stela; he gave to her a new divine offering, and he built her a temple of stone, renewing what he had found, namely these gods in her place.

Live Horus, the Mezer, the King of Upper and Lower Egypt, Khufu, given life. He found the house of Isis, Mistress of the Pyramid, by the side of the hollow of Hwran [The Sphinx] . . . and he built his pyramid beside the temple of this goddess and he built a pyramid for the King's daughter Henutsen beside this temple.

The place of Hwran Hor-em-akhet is on the South side of the House of Isis, Mistress of the pyramid and on the north of Osiris, Lord of Rostaw. The plans of the image of Hor-em-akhet were brought in order to bring to revision the sayings of the disposition of the Image of the Very Redoubtable.

He restored the statue all covered in painting, of the Guardian of the Atmosphere, who guides the winds with his gaze. He made to quarry the hind part of the nemes headdress, which was lacking, from gilded stone, and which had a length of about 7 ells (3.70 meters).

He came to make a tour, in order to see the thunderbolt, which stands in the place of the Sycamore, so named because of a great sycamore, whose branches were struck when the Lord of Heaven descended upon the place of Hor-em-akhet, and also this image, retracing the erasure according to the above-mentioned disposition. . . .

The figure of this god, cut in stone, is solid and will last to eternity, keeping its face looking always to the Orient.[17]

In the above passage we are told that Khufu made repairs to the Sphinx, thus implying that the Sphinx was already of considerable age by the time of Khufu and, by extension, the time of his son Khafre, the king who is believed by those of conventional opinion—based on highly contentious circumstantial evidence—to have constructed the monument.

Conventional Egyptology gives little credence to this contradictory ancient Egyptian text, believing it to be the work of pious priests of the Saite Period (ca. 685–525 BCE) in order to legitimize their rule. But regardless of the Egyptologists' protestations, the actual evidence onsite at Giza seems to support this ancient text (i.e., that Khufu was indeed making repairs to various monuments at Giza). Specifically named are the Sphinx and the Temple of Isis, which is interesting, because this, of course, implies that, contrary to mainstream opinion, the cult of Osiris/Isis was already highly developed (Isis being referred to as a goddess and Osiris as lord) as early as the Fourth Dynasty (if not before).

But where's the physical evidence to support the claims made on the Inventory Stele? In the 1930s, when Egyptologist Selim Hassan, Ph.D., was clearing away the sands that had long since engulfed the Sphinx, he discovered that ancient repair works had indeed been made to the head of the Sphinx and that the dimension of the repair work he observed closely matched the dimension given in the Inventory Stele—3.7 meters. Hassan also noted that a sycamore tree was growing slightly to the south of the Sphinx and, given that these trees can live for thousands of years, surmised that it may have been an offshoot of the original sycamore mentioned in the Inventory Stele that had been struck with a bolt of lightning. Furthermore, traces of ancient paint (also mentioned in the Inventory Stele) have also been found on the side of the Sphinx's head. So it seems that—far from being a "pious fraud"—the Inventory Stele clearly makes a number of statements of proven historical fact, and this must surely confer credibility and authenticity on the testimony of the Inventory Stele as a whole.

Given such incontrovertible facts, it is somewhat surprising then to find that Egyptologists continue to deny the veracity of the Inventory Stele's "testimony." Here we have an ancient text that speaks of (at least four) verifiable facts written in a very matter-of-fact manner, yet, simply because this text makes one remark that is inconsistent with the views of conventional Egyptology (i.e., Khufu repaired the Sphinx), the entire content of the Inventory Stele is regarded by Egyptologists not as fact but as more of a lie and is to be dismissed and ignored.

In short, verifiable fact after verifiable fact is presented in the text of the Inventory Stele, just not (according to Egyptologists) the remark that Khufu repaired the Sphinx. It seems that rather than change their own narrative, Egyptologists would rather dismiss the historical evidence that contradicts it, as if the Saite Period priests somehow conspired to write only verifiable facts about the Sphinx that did not concern its age or provenance. In this Egyptologists claim to know better than the ancient Egyptians themselves, the ancient Egyptians who were nearer to and who would have had better access to both oral and written traditions that are perhaps now long since lost and forgotten.

To justify their dismissal of this ancient text, Egyptologists point to its orthography—that the Inventory Stele is clearly written in the language of the Saite Period, about 1,800 years after the Fourth Dynasty, and that it also makes mention of a number of Egyptian deities that did not exist in the Fourth Dynasty. But as West remarks, "To dismiss it [the information within the Inventory Stele] because of its Late Kingdom date is like having only a 20th Century translation of the Bible available and concluding from that, that the Bible is a 20th century document because of the language."[18]

West makes a perfectly valid point; the Inventory Stele could very well be a Saite Period reproduction of a much older text, written in the style of the Saite Period and updating the names of the ancient gods with their Saite Period equivalents in much the same way that, for example, the later Greek god Hermes had usurped the powers and name of the much earlier Egyptian god Thoth.

If it is evidence that counts then it seems, at least to me, that there exists considerable evidence that contradicts the conventional dating of these monuments. But if these structures *are* older than their conventional dating, then how much older are they?

ARK OF AGES

In *The Giza Prophecy,* I showed how the pyramids at Giza and the Sphinx worked together to present a great, stellar timepiece—a "precession clock." By using the stars of Orion's Belt and presenting to us their maximum and minimum culminations at each end of the precession time line (figure 7.4 on page 162), the builders were able to calibrate their time line and, with the use of the Sphinx, mark a fairly specific date on the time line relative to our present time—circa 3980 BCE.

To understand how the precession time line in figure 7.4 works, imagine that you draw a straight line on the ground about a foot or so in length. At one end of your line you place a marker, "12:00 p.m.," and at the opposite end of your line you place another marker, "12:00 a.m." You now have a time line of twenty-four-hours duration (i.e., twelve hours in one direction and twelve hours in the return direction).

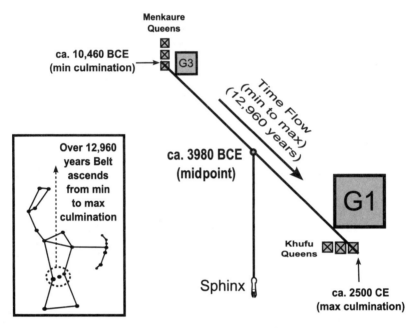

Giza - Orion Precession Timeline   N→

Figure 7.4. Giza-Orion precession time line (ca. 10,460 BCE–ca. 2500 CE). Precession is moving from minimum culmination toward maximum culmination. Image by Scott Creighton.

In front of your line you place a simple pendulum. As the pendulum swings back and forth, with each swing it will pass over every point on the time line—every hour, minute and second. And it will cover each point on the time line *twice*—once on the *outward* swing and then again on the *return* swing to complete one full cycle.

To then highlight the specific time of 6:00 a.m. on the time line, all you would need to do is place a marker of some kind at the precise midpoint of your time line, because 6:00 a.m. is precisely midway (50 percent) between 12:00 a.m. and 12:00 p.m. (figure 7.5). Then, simple calculations (length of time line divided by 720 minutes in half a day) will allow the time at *any* point that happened to be indicated on the time line (with the placement of a marker of some kind) to be correctly

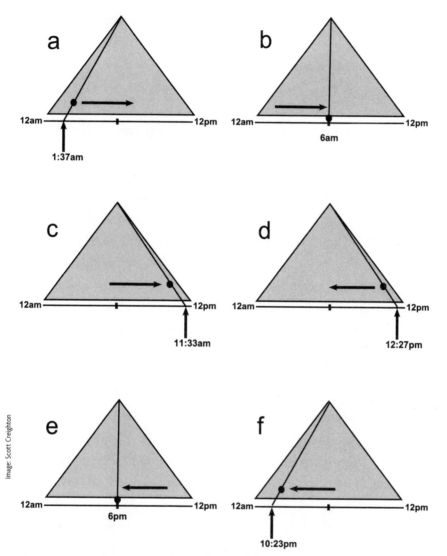

Figure 7.5. Pendulum time line. The pendulum bob passes over each point of the time line twice; once on the outward swing and then again on the return swing. To know whether, for example, the midpoint is aligned to 6:00 a.m. or 6:00 p.m. requires us to know the direction of the swing.

calculated. Of course, the midpoint can be 6:00 a.m. or 6:00 p.m. To determine whether the marked time is 6:00 a.m. or 6:00 p.m. requires us to know the *direction* of the pendulum swing (i.e., the motion of time).

And this is precisely what we are presented with at Giza, although, rather than marking the end points of the time line with 12:00 a.m. and 12:00 p.m. (a twenty-four-hour day), the precession time line uses the Earth's much longer precessional cycle (i.e., the 25,920-year Great Year). In this Great Year the particular orientation of the belt stars at their precessional *maximum* culmination can be likened to the 12:00 p.m. marker in our pendulum example, while the particular orientation of the belt stars at their precessional *minimum* culmination can be likened to the opposite 12:00 a.m. marker.

The analogy of the pendulum bob and its time line is precisely the same with the precession time line at Giza except that the motion of the pendulum bob is replaced by the imperceptibly slow precessional motion (pendulum swing) of the belt stars and particularly Al Nitak. During a full precessional cycle of 25,920 years (i.e., from maximum to minimum culmination and then back again), each point along the Giza precession time line will correspond to a particular position of Orion's Belt within its actual precessional cycle. And just like the pendulum bob, when the belt stars reach one of their two culmination points, they will appear to momentarily stop and then begin to move in the *opposite direction*. This change of precessional direction of the belt stars means that the precessional motion will then retrace its 12,960-year journey back along the Giza precession time line (the *return* swing of the pendulum), thereby corresponding with each point along the precession time line a *second* time.

In our example of the precession time line in figure 7.4, we see that the Sphinx is aligned to the significant midpoint of the precession time line at circa 3980 BCE (ca. 3980 BCE being the most *recent* midpoint date of Orion's precessional half-cycle). But as can be seen in the pendulum example (figure 7.5), the pendulum bob in one full day passes the six o'clock position *twice* (as it does with *all* time positions on the time line). How then do we know if this six o'clock is indicating 6:00 p.m. or if it is twelve hours previous; that is, 6:00 a.m.? Similarly, how do we know if this significant midpoint on the Giza time line that the Sphinx is aligned to is indicating circa 3980 BCE and not the *previous* midpoint date of circa 16,940 BCE (one half-cycle of 12,960 years previous; that is, 3,980 + 12,960 years; figure 7.6)?

And therein lies the problem; how can we actually know which of the previous midpoint alignments the builders are actually referring to? Does the midpoint indicate—allegorically speaking—6:00 a.m. or 6:00 p.m. (figure 7.5)? Was the Sphinx midpoint alignment first made to indicate the time circa 3980 BCE (the most recent midpoint alignment date; figure 7.4), thereby suggesting the structures were created around that time, or is the Sphinx midpoint alignment indicating the half-cycle *before* circa 3980 BCE (i.e., ca. 16,940 BCE; figure 7.6), thereby suggesting the pyramids are of much greater antiquity? In short, is the most recent midpoint alignment (ca. 3980 BCE) the *outward* or the *return* swing of the precession pendulum?

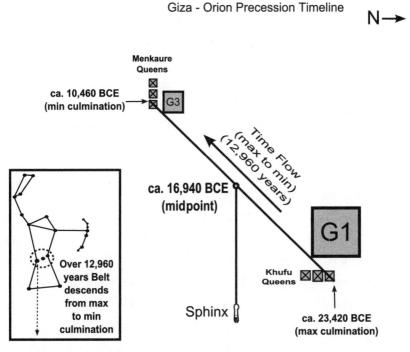

Figure 7.6. Giza-Orion precession time line (ca. 23,420 BCE–ca. 10,460 BCE). Precession is moving from maximum culmination toward minimum culmination. Image by Scott Creighton (derivative of original by Gary Osborn).

Alas, there is no easy way to tell. Without knowing the initial direction time was flowing when the Giza precession time line was created, we are reduced to guesswork.

Unless, of course, the builders somehow found a clever and logical way of encoding the direction that time was flowing into the layout of this great precession timepiece at the time of its creation at Giza. But is such a means possible? Could the architect have found a way to encode such a crucial piece of information into the Giza precession time line?

There is a possibility.

The reader may recall from chapter 3 how the three main pyramids at Giza may have been designed using the geo-stellar fingerprint of the Orion's Belt stars (figure 3.3a–d, pages 66 and 68). We see that the starting point for this design *begins* by extending an initial line from the G1/Al Nitak center to the G2/Al Nilam center. It is reasonable to suggest then that G1 represents the *starting* point of the full precessional cycle (i.e., the initial outward swing of the precessional pendulum), because the design of the Giza pyramids commences from G1/Al Nitak.

Conversely, if the flow of time had been moving from the *opposite* end of the Giza precession time line (i.e., from G3 toward G1; figure 7.4), then the geo-stellar fingerprint would have commenced with a line from the G3/Mintaka center to the G2/Al Nilam center, thereby creating three pyramid bases of very different shapes and proportions to what we actually have at Giza today (figure 7.7).

This is to say that commencing the design of the geo-stellar fingerprint of Orion's Belt with an initial line drawn from the Al Nitak center to the Al Nilam center (figure 3.3a–d) (i.e., from the maximum [G1] to minimum [G3] culmination) will produce—to a high degree of accuracy—the relative proportions of the main Giza pyramids, thereby suggesting that the Orion geo-stellar fingerprint serves to "lock in" the direction in which time was initially flowing along the precession time line at the time of its creation.

In summary, the geo-stellar fingerprint of Orion's Belt, in providing three bases whose relative proportions are dependent on the direction

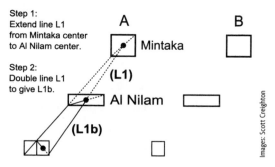

Images: Scott Creighton

*Figure 7.7. (A) By commencing the geo-stellar fingerprint technique by
extending a line from Mintaka (top star) to Al Nilam (middle star) of
Orion's Belt, we end up with three bases of varying dimensions.
(B) These bases in no way agree with the relative proportions
of the three square bases of the Giza pyramids.*

from which the design commences, provides us with a very clever and
foolproof means of determining from which end of the Giza precession
time line the outward pendulum swing commenced; the direction of
the geo-stellar design (starting at G1/Al Nitak) may have been used in
order to present to us the direction of the time flow (i.e., from G1/Al
Nitak toward G3/Mintaka).

Thus, if we are to commence the outward swing of time on the
Giza precession time line from the direction of G1, then, logically,
this implies that G1's three queens represent the *previous* maximum
culmination of 23,420 BCE since the *next* maximum culmination of
Orion's Belt (i.e., when the flow of time on the Giza precession time
line will change direction again and move from G1 toward G3) hasn't
yet occurred and won't occur until circa 2500 CE—a little under five
hundred years from now. And it logically follows that if the Giza precession time line is calibrated by the two culminations of Orion's Belt
of circa 23,420 BCE (maximum) and circa 10,460 BCE (minimum)
then the Sphinx is aligned to the midpoint of the precession time line,
circa 16,940 BCE (as opposed to the *next* midpoint alignment some
12,960 years later, circa 3980 BCE).

And perhaps this is also why this configuration of pyramids at Giza produces the Great Giza Triangle (figure 2.2 on page 37) that points *away* from Khufu's pyramid (and its queens' maximum culmination markers) *toward* Menkaure's pyramid (and its queens' minimum culmination markers), thereby suggesting again that the direction or outward swing of time on the Giza precession time line was initially moving from maximum culmination toward minimum culmination, thus supporting the idea that the outward swing or starting point of the precessional cycle was circa 23,420 BCE.

Another important point that should be noted here is the fact that the Sphinx, as noted already, is aligned precisely to the significant midpoint of the precession time line. If this alignment of the Sphinx to the midpoint of the Giza precession time line was created to indicate that some significant event occurred around this midpoint time, then we have to ask, just how likely is it that a significant event just happened to occur at the precise midpoint of the precession time line as indicated by the Sphinx? Is this just some extraordinary coincidence, that a significant event should occur at the precise midpoint on the time line, or is there perhaps a more rational explanation for such a correlation?

It is probably no coincidence. What we have to keep in mind here is that the designers of this great precession time line at Giza set out to mark a very specific moment in time and that they planned to do this using a linear time line (as opposed to our modern circular analog clock). In planning their time line the designers would have understood that any line has three obvious significant points—its beginning, middle, and end. By designing their linear time line around these three significant points they would effectively be highlighting the significance (and nonrandomness) of what they had designed by the very fact that they had chosen to use the three significant points of their time line. This is to say that by using the three significant points on their time line the designers could effectively demonstrate that such an arrangement was not a chance occurrence, that it had been very carefully thought out and executed.

But to use and mark the significant midpoint of the time line (with the Sphinx) would require that at the date this significant event occurred, the designers would need to identify a star (or group of stars) that was precisely at the midpoint of its precessional half-cycle. In selecting such a group of stars the designers could then align their marker (the Sphinx) to the significant midpoint of the Giza time line. The beginning and end of the precession time line would then be marked with culmination markers displaying the minimum and maximum culminations of the chosen star group (i.e., their 12:00 a.m. and 12:00 p.m. positions).

Because all stars in the night sky reach their culminations at different times throughout the Great Year (thereby reaching their precessional half-cycle midpoints at different times), the designers would have had relatively few obvious stars (or groups of stars) to choose from, and it just so happened that circa 3980 BCE, when the significant event occurred (or perhaps a half-cycle earlier, ca. 16,940 BCE), Orion's Belt just happened to be precisely at the midpoint of its precessional journey, and the rest, as they say, is history.

In short, choosing and presenting a star (Al Nitak in Orion's Belt) that was at the middle of its precessional half-cycle allowed the designers to highlight (with the Sphinx) the significant midpoint on the Giza precession time line, thereby displaying intent, meaning, and purpose; this was no chance occurrence. This is to say that Orion's Belt was probably selected by the designers of the precession time line for no other reason than the fact that these stars just happened to be midway through their precessional half-cycle at the very time the designers were seeking such a group of stars (i.e., when a significant Earth event occurred). And with the choice of Orion's Belt to calibrate the precession time line, the Orion's Belt stars would then become identified with the body of Osiris (i.e., the sixteen pyramid arks that represented the dismembered body of Osiris). Orion's Belt (or at least Al Nitak), would become the stellar personification of the great god Osiris, known to the ancient Egyptians as *Sah*.

What all of this suggests, of course, is that we may well have been presented with a means of dating these monuments far beyond the

present precessional half-cycle and that we may well be looking at structures at Giza (and elsewhere in Egypt) that are very much older than conventional thought would ever have us believe, even though the ancient
Egyptians *themselves* told us that their civilization was tens of thousands
of years older than is presently accepted in conventional circles.

EARTH'S CHANGING POLE

So what does all of this mean, and what relevance does it have to the
key question of this chapter—deluge and drought? Simple. One of the
most extraordinary and single most devastating events ever to have
occurred within the past twenty thousand years on this planet is the
relatively sudden and inexplicable meltdown of the great Laurentide and
Cordilleran Ice Sheets—an event whose start coincides very well with
the midpoint of the precession time line (i.e., the *previous* half-cycle)
circa 16,940 BCE (around nineteen thousand years ago).

Did something happen circa 16,940 BCE to trigger the termination of the Ice Age? Did our ancient forebears witness something in the
heavens—a displacement of the stars (thereby the Earth's pole)—during
this distant epoch that brought them to conclude that a great deluge
was imminent? And did they take measures in that remote epoch circa
16,940 BCE to attempt to save their world from the ever-rising global
seas? Is *this* when they first built their great pyramid arks?

Many researchers and writers both past and present have often speculated that the sudden termination and (relatively) rapid meltdown of
the great ice sheets that once covered North America and Europe some
twenty thousand years ago resulted from a sudden and dramatic change
in the geographic location of the Earth's pole, a shift of the polar axis
that displaced the great ice sheets into warmer latitudes, where they
received more solar radiation from the sun, causing them to go in to
relatively rapid meltdown.

Most modern scientists, however, dismiss such dramatic pole shifts as
impossible, insisting that the Earth's equatorial bulge is simply too great a

stabilizing influence for the Earth's polar axis to be rapidly altered in any significant way. At the same time, however, science *does* accept that the Earth's polar axis can—and does—change its location (albeit very slowly) by around 1 degree every million years. This imperceptibly slow geographic relocation of the Earth's polar axis is known as true polar wander.

True polar wander does not require the Earth itself to tilt nor does it require the Earth's crust to slide over the inner lithosphere, as in Earth crust displacement theory. To understand true polar wander, we can imagine a ball of plasticine with a rod pushed through its center, representing the Earth's axis of rotation. We can then draw horizontal lines around the ball (i.e., perpendicular to the rod) representing lines of latitude. If you then tilt the rod forward, the entire ball will tilt with the rod. In such a tilt all latitudes remain exactly the same distance from the pole as before, although some latitudes will have tilted more toward the sun and will receive more solar radiation, while other latitudes will have done the opposite.

Now imagine a scenario whereby the plasticine ball stays in place but the rod (i.e., the polar axis) slides through the plasticine ball to another location. This is true polar wander, and it results in latitude changes because some latitudes will now be nearer to the rod (the pole) while others will be farther away, resulting in a changed geographic location (relative to the pole) and, consequently, a changed climate to just about every place on the planet.

But what if true polar wander could occur at a much faster rate than ever thought possible? This is essentially the theory put forward by physicists W. Woelfli and W. Baltensperger, who write:

A rapid geographical shift of the poles is physically possible. At present, the Earth is in hydrostatic equilibrium. Since it rotates, its radius is larger at the equator (by 21 km) than at the poles. The rotational motion of an object is governed by its inertial tensor. In a coordinate system fixed to the object and with the origin at the center of mass, this tensor is obtained by an integration over the density times a bilinear expression of the cartesian components. At present, due to the equatorial bulge, one of the main axes of Earth's inertial tensor is longer than the other two, and its direction coincides with that of the rotation axis. This is a stable situation. For a polar shift, a further deformation of the Earth is required. The ensuing motion leads to new geographic positions of the North and South Poles.

During the shift, the direction of the angular momentum vector remains strictly fixed relative to the stars, as required by conservation laws. What turns is the globe relative to the rotation axis.[19]

In an accompanying paper, the same physicists also write the following:

As is well known, during the Last Glacial Maximum, about 20,000 years ago, the ice was asymmetrically distributed around the present North Pole. It reached the region of New York, while east Siberia remained ice free. Mammoths lived in arctic regions of east Siberia, where now their food cannot grow. Therefore the globe must have been turned in such a way that the North Pole was in Greenland.

The required rapid geographic pole shift at the end of the ice ages has been shown to be physically possible, on condition that an astronomical object of planetary size in an extremely eccentric orbit existed.[20]

Essentially the rapid true polar wander described by Woelfli and Baltensperger commenced from near central Greenland, which, about twenty thousand years ago, happened to be the approximate geographic center of the massive ice sheets at their maximum extent. As the Greenland pole rapidly migrated northward, it did so in a spiral fashion (figure 7.8), eventually coming to settle at its present location, around 18 degrees (1,253 miles) farther north in the Arctic Sea. This migration of the pole resulted in a relative displacement of the great ice sheets farther southward into much warmer latitudes. Naturally, the same would

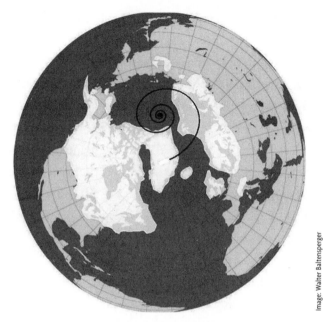

Image: Walter Baltensperger

*Figure 7.8. The former Greenland pole migrates in a
spiral fashion to the present Arctic Sea pole.*

also be true of the South Pole in Antarctica, which would have been displaced by the same amount.

The intriguing aspect of this proposed shift of the pole by around 18 degrees from central Greenland to the Arctic Sea is the effect a relocation of this magnitude of the pole would have had at Giza and the possibility that this effect seems to have been recorded in the Great Pyramid. As stated, different parts of the globe would be displaced or relocated by differing degrees, so, while the pole itself was relocated by around 18 degrees from central Greenland to the Arctic Sea, at Giza (as a result of the Earth's rotational axis of 23.5°), the latitudinal relocation would only have been around 6 degrees (figure 7.9).

Giza is presently almost exactly 60 degrees distant from the present Arctic Sea pole (4,158 miles). However, when the pole was centered in Greenland, as proposed by Woelfli and Baltensperger, Giza was then only around 54 degrees (3,736 miles) from the pole (i.e., Giza was around 6° nearer to the pole in relative latitude, at around 36° N). However, as the pole rapidly migrated to the Arctic Sea (in its spiral motion), Giza's relative latitude to the migrating pole would have fluctuated, at times being closer and at other times being farther away from the pole. This fluctuation would, of course, have had serious environmental consequences on the ground, causing the climate in Egypt and the wider Near East (and, indeed, all over the planet) to fluctuate wildly between wet and arid conditions until, eventually, the pole settled in the Arctic Sea, leaving Giza high and dry at 30 degrees N latitude—a relative latitudinal relocation of some 6 degrees nearer to the equator from its former latitude of around 36 degrees N.

But what evidence is there that the ancient Egyptians actually observed this 6-degree change in the latitude of Giza? Such a relocation of the Earth's polar axis would, naturally, have had reciprocal con-

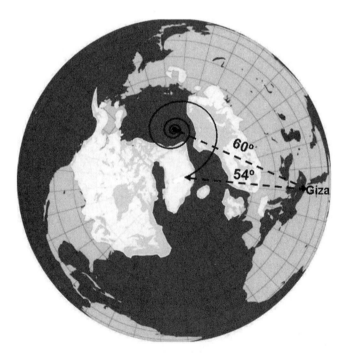

Figure 7.9. Giza was formerly only 54° from the Greenland pole
but is now 60° distant. Image by Scott Creighton
(based on original by Walter Baltensperger).

sequences in the heavens; to a ground-based observer, the stars would appear to have changed their relative positions in response to the relocated rotational axis of the Earth.

It is a curious thing that around the midpoint of the Giza precession time line (ca. 16,940 BCE; around 19,000 BP), the star Al Nitak in Orion's Belt (the Great Pyramid's stellar counterpart) would have reached a maximum altitude on the meridian (due south) of around 39 degrees above the local horizon. Now, if the Earth's polar axis had been relocated at this time from central Greenland to the Arctic Sea (an 18 degrees relocation of the pole), then this would have resulted in the star Al Nitak appearing (from the latitude of Giza) to have rapidly risen from an altitude of around 39 degrees on the southern meridian up to an altitude of around 45 degrees. And quite remarkably, this shift in altitude of Al Nitak from an altitude of around 39 degrees up to an altitude of around 45 degrees (a shift of some 6°) seems to have been recorded within the star shafts of the Great Pyramid (figure 7.10).

In the diagram in figure 7.10, we observe that the Great Pyramid's

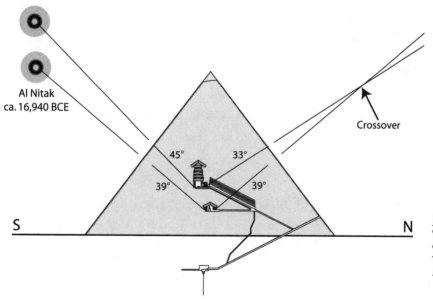

Figure 7.10. The shafts of the Great Pyramid indicate a 6° shift in the altitude of Al Nitak in Orion's Belt.

stellar counterpart, Al Nitak in Orion's Belt, is targeted by the *southern shaft* of the Queen's Chamber at an angle of around 39 degrees (its preshift altitude when the pole was in central Greenland). The northern shaft of the Queen's Chamber targets Al Nitak's "mirror position" in the northern sky, also at an altitude of around 39 degrees. When we now consider the southern shaft of the King's Chamber we find that it targets Al Nitak at an altitude of around 45 degrees (its postshift altitude with the pole now relocated 18 degrees north to its present location in the Arctic Sea). This represents a rise in altitude of Al Nitak of some 6 degrees ($39° + 6° = 45°$) and is what we would expect to observe at Giza as a result of an 18 degrees or so relocation of the pole from central Greenland to the Arctic Sea. Conversely, the northern "mirror shaft" of the King's Chamber *drops* from the northern "mirror shaft" in the Queen's Chamber by 6 degrees to around 33 degrees altitude ($39° − 6° = 33°$).

In addition, that we actually observe that the trajectories of the northern shafts cross over, while the southern shaft trajectories do not, is exactly what we might expect of a "heavens in motion" scenario; that is, the Earth's polar axis migrating to a new geographical location, thereby giving the appearance to a ground-based observer that the stars themselves were departing from their normal course. Indeed, had the Earth's polar axis migrated in the *opposite* direction (from the Arctic Sea to central Greenland) then we would have found that it was the southern shaft trajectories that crossed over, while the northern shaft trajectories did not. This is to say that the builders would have constructed the star shafts the precise opposite to how they are today.

In short, the shift of the heavens at Giza by 6 degrees as shown by the four star shafts of the Great Pyramid would seem to corroborate the 18-degree shift of the Earth's polar axis from Central Greenland to the Arctic Sea, as proposed by the research of Woelfli and Baltensperger. And, of course, if this is correct, it provides evidence that the Giza pyramids are much older than conventional Egyptology would have us believe and of which—as has been shown—some physical evidence suggests.

And how extraordinary is it that one precessional half-cycle later, circa 3,980 BCE, *another* natural disaster seems to have occurred in Egypt that, if the research of Australian astronomer George F. Dodwell is correct, also seems to have involved a disturbance of the Earth's polar axis, an event that brought about a drought so severe that the kingdom of ancient Egypt would eventually collapse.[21] Were the early, giant pyramids, as some evidence suggests, merely repaired by the Egyptians of this later period in anticipation of the second strike of the clock when Al Nitak made its second pass (its return swing) through the significant midpoint of the Giza precession time line, the flipside of the great deluge—a deadly drought?

Deluge and drought—two halves of the same significant midpoint on the Giza precessional time line, circa 16,940 BCE and circa 3980 BCE. Might this perhaps also explain why the Sphinx has the head of a man (symbolizing the age of Aquarius/water, circa 23,420 BCE) while having also the body of a lion (symbolizing the age of Leo/fire ca. 10,460 BCE)? Aquarius and Leo. Water and fire. Deluge and drought. Endless cycles of natural destruction whose pivotal moments—the midpoints between the two ages of Leo and Aquarius—may have been marked out for us on the ground at Giza in a great precession time line and perhaps also in the form of the Sphinx, which indicates these two ages.

ARK FOR ART'S SAKE

Many will be familiar with the biblical story of Noah and the Flood. But there are numerous similar stories from cultures all around the world whereby a good and righteous man is forewarned of an impending deluge that is to be sent forth by God or the gods in order to "cleanse" the world and he is told to build an ark in order to salvage a remnant of humanity (and other creatures).

In medieval art Noah's Ark is typically portrayed as some kind of massive wooden boat, sometimes with multiple decks (see figure 7.11 on page 178), but, curiously, this is not how the Ark was always perceived or portrayed in art.

Photo: Giovanni Dall'Orto

Figure 7.11. Animals enter Noah's Ark, Aurelio Luini, 1555.

The bronze panel in figure 7.12 that depicts Noah's Ark and the Flood comes from the Gates of Paradise doors on Italy's Florence Baptistery. The doors were designed by Lorenzo Ghiberti in the fifteenth century; the images depict a series of biblical events. As Gwynne Ann Dilbeck notes in her art history dissertation:

> Origen's homilies were incorporated into the lectionaries of Renaissance Florence for use in liturgical services. In addition, his understanding that Noah's Ark took the form of a pyramid informs the shape of the Ark in Ghiberti's Noah panel.
>
> The panel of Noah does not portray the more common image of the Flood, which seems strange given that the Flood is interpreted as a parallel to the sacrament of baptism. However, in Ghiberti's narrative panel the waters have receded, leaving the past washed away. In the middle section the family and animals of Noah are represented

Figure 7.12. Depiction of Lorenzo Ghiberti's Noah and the Flood *from the Gates of Paradise in the Florence Baptistery, Italy. Pyramid outline enhanced by Scott Creighton to original photo by Ricardo André Frantz.*

exiting the Ark, which takes the form of a pyramid [figure 7.12]. Their salvation is underlined by the dead body lying at their feet. The two scenes in the foreground depict Noah's sacrifice and his drunkenness. The sloping sides of the Ark serve to frame and draw attention to the foreground scenes, and the three episodes themselves form a pyramid in the composition.[22]

The pyramid shape of the Ark may refer directly to Origen's interpretation of the Ark. Again, according to Dilbeck, "Origen, an Egyptian

Photo: The Yorck Project

Figure 7.13. Paolo Uccello's Flood and Waters Subsiding. *Note the square lower bases of the pyramids with their slightly sloping sides.*

Father of the Church, envisioned the Ark as a truncated pyramid with three decks . . . all of the earlier writers thought of it [the Ark] as pyramidal in shape. . . . Uccello's Ark is also a pyramid."[23]

Photos: Scott Creighton

Figure 7.14. Boat pits beside Great Pyramid

It seems quite clear then that among some early Christian scholars and artists there existed a tradition that the ark that had saved humanity from the biblical Flood took the form not of a giant, wooden boat, but of giant pyramids, although, it has to be said, the giant pyramids were themselves surrounded by boats set into giant boat pits (figure 7.14).

Where would such an idea have come from? Perhaps these early writers and artists had access to ancient texts, now long since lost, that described the early, giant Egyptian pyramids in precisely such terms—as arks.

8
Flying Stones

That something was lost from the time of the pyramid building age up to this present era is certain; otherwise, why is it that not a single scholar—whether associated with the field of physics, engineering, archaeology, Egyptology, mathematics, geometry or scores of others—can conclusively state exactly how the mighty pyramids were built?

J. P. Lepre, *The Egyptian Pyramids*

While the primary focus of this book has concerned itself with the *why* question of the pyramids—why they were built—the other inter-related question that puzzles the minds of many is the *how* question: How exactly did the ancient Egyptians build these colossal structures, and how were they able to achieve the construction of so many (around sixteen) in such a relatively short period of time—around one hundred years?

It is a question that has perplexed and befuddled the greatest minds in Egyptology (and beyond) for centuries: How did people, not long out of the Stone Age, manage to quarry, move, and lift millions of 2.5-ton limestone blocks and numerous 70-ton granite blocks to heights of a little under five hundred feet to construct their pyramids? Suffice to say that there have been many proposals: some straightforward such as the conventional ramp theory (interior or exterior), and others that are rather more exotic such as some form of counterweight system or cast blocks, to the truly bizarre theories such as UFOs, sonic levitation devices, hydraulic locks, and the like.

If, however, we approach the problem here on the premise that the ancient Egyptians believed that they had limited time (the Arab chronicles tell us three hundred years) in which to devise and implement a recovery plan for their kingdom before it would be decimated in a great deluge and drought, we can get a sense of the urgency with which the ancient Egyptians would likely have approached their Project Osiris.

For such a project to succeed, for such a mighty endeavor, they would have had to mobilize the entire population over many generations. They would have had to succeed in doing things that no one in history had ever before achieved. This would have required the development of an infrastructure to manage and support the massive numbers of people involved in the project, to feed and house them, to attend to their injuries and other human needs. Skills and technologies in the cutting, transporting, lifting, and dressing of vast quantities of stone (limestone and granite) would have had to be developed.

In short, this enterprise was for the ancient Egyptians of this remote period every bit as challenging and daunting as our own twentieth-century "space race" and President John F. Kennedy's goal of placing a man on the moon (and maybe more so). As a result of Kennedy's pledge, wider society would ultimately benefit and progress as a direct result of the various technologies that had to be invented in order for the moon mission to succeed. And the ancient Egyptians' race to implement their Project Osiris would, for this age, produce many world firsts and remarkable feats of engineering, and they would achieve all of this because they simply *had* to; failure was not an option. Necessity is, after all, the mother of invention.

One of the first decisions the ancient Egyptians would have been faced with in implementing their recovery project was deciding exactly what to build: What form should the recovery system—their arks—take? This decision would be governed primarily by two quite important requirements:

1. The arks would have to be so large as to be visible for many miles in every direction, thus facilitating their relatively easy and quick discovery.
2. The arks would have to be so strong and durable as to be able to withstand the tremendous forces of nature (the deluge) that the builders anticipated they would have to withstand.

It would have been quickly realized that a pyramid was the only suitable structure they could build, because in ancient times without iron or steel a structure wider at the bottom and narrower at the top was the most stable structure that could have been built to a sufficient height to satisfy the requirement of high visibility from great distances. It would have been realized also that the planned pyramids would have to be constructed of stone since the mud-brick structures that had been built previously would simply be washed away in the anticipated deluge.

Time was also a constraining factor; the recovery plan had to be implemented as quickly as possible. One of the things this time constraint would have an impact on would be the size of the stone blocks used to build the pyramids. If the blocks were made very small then this would require much more cutting and thereby would require much more time. So, to save time, it was necessary to keep the blocks fairly large. However, if the blocks were made too large then they would become too difficult or impossible to move and maneuver. In short, the blocks couldn't be too small (as this would take too long to cut them) and neither could they be too large (as this would make them too difficult to move). So, in order to use average-size blocks weighing around 2.5 tons, a means had to be found that would allow the ancient

Egyptians to quickly and easily lift and maneuver such heavy blocks.

In this regard it stands to reason that the builders could only have developed a lifting technology that was wholly within their reach. We need not invoke or invite some exotic science into this particular question, of which there is little, if any, evidence. Whatever means the ancient Egyptians employed to move these heavy blocks should, in theory at least, have been entirely within their grasp, have left behind some physical evidence of its use, and perhaps even some written evidence.

As far as conventional Egyptology is concerned the technology employed by the ancient builders to raise these heavy blocks was the ramp—massive ramps that would be built either straight onto the pyramid face or perhaps coiled around the pyramid slopes. However, the evidence for the use of such massive external ramps envisaged by Egyptologists is entirely threadbare, and depending on the particular ramp envisaged, such a technique would bring with it its own physical and logistical problems. And while there is indeed some evidence of ramps or dirt transport roads at a number of pyramid sites (mostly from later periods), these would appear only to have been for ancillary purposes such as hauling cut stone blocks out of the quarries and up to the base of the pyramid. There are no massive construction ramps still extant at any of the pyramids and little sign that any such massive ramps ever existed.

The issue of building massive ramps in order to construct the pyramids also brings in the issue of time constraint into the equation. In the case of the early, giant pyramids this would have been a very considerable undertaking whereby the construction of the ramp itself would have been almost as massive a construction project as the building of the pyramid. In this regard, Lehner writes, "Given the fact that the stones of a giant pyramid like Khufu's had to be raised as much as 146m (479 ft) from the ground, if a ramp was indeed used it would have been a colossal structure in its own right. According to some ideas about its shape, it would in fact have required as much or more material than the pyramid itself."[1]

If time was such a constraint as seems likely, it would seem then that the ancient builders would have been required to become much more inventive, that, by necessity, they would have had to discover some other technology that would negate the necessity for the construction of massive, time-consuming ramps but, at the same time, enable the raising of these heavy blocks in a much easier and more time-efficient manner. They would have needed to discover a lifting technology that was scalable and was available to them almost from day one rather than expending many years and much effort building massive ramps and then rebuilding them as the pyramid gradually rose in height. But what lifting technology might they have discovered that would allow them to achieve all this that would be scalable and available to them virtually from day one?

A clue to this might exist in one of the oldest legends that speak of how the ancient Egyptians (and other pyramid builders around the world) built their giant pyramids; these legends tell us that the builders "flew the stones into place."

Now, on the surface most of us would be inclined to immediately dismiss such a legend as entirely fanciful (if not downright ludicrous), and especially so when some individuals attempt to explain this legend by invoking the use of sonic levitation devices that somehow managed to neutralize gravitational forces, thereby rendering the great limestone and granite blocks entirely weightless.

The fact is, however, that such exotic science has never been proved. No one in modern times has yet demonstrated that limestone and granite blocks can be rendered entirely weightless with such exotic techniques, and until someone *can* demonstrate how a seventy-ton granite block can be rendered entirely weightless using such a technique, then such notions must remain in the realm of fiction.

But perhaps all is not lost. If there does exist an essence of truth to this ancient legend of the limestone and granite blocks being "flown into place" on the pyramid, then surely we must seek a much less exotic means of achieving such a feat. This, of course, implies that the ancient

Egyptians perhaps discovered and applied another, less exotic (but easily accessible) technology that *could* have rendered these heavy blocks "weightless," thus making "flying blocks" a possibility and thus perhaps explaining the legend of the "flying stones" that has come down to us.

Such a technology that *would* have been at the disposal of the ancient Egyptian builders (were they only to have discovered it) is the power and application of thermodynamics. In short, might the ancient Egyptians have discovered the power of hot air contained in some form of envelope or balloon?

Fanciful?

Perhaps. The hot air balloon was, according to conventional historians, supposedly only invented in the eighteenth century CE, so to advocate such an extraordinary idea that so contradicts conventional thought surely requires that such a notion be backed up with some extraordinary evidence. However, while extraordinary evidence may be in absentia, before we dismiss the idea completely out of hand let us consider some potential evidence that *could* in fact lend support to such an extraordinary possibility.

First of all, it is not at all difficult to observe how hot air produces "lift," and we should realize that this phenomenon would have been as easy to observe by ancient people as it is for us to observe today. In the late eighteenth century the Montgolfier brothers, Joseph and Jacques, noticed how when they burned paper (which they manufactured) the ashes floated up into the air. What caused this? they wondered. The Montgolfier brothers believed that heat and smoke had some peculiar property that could lift things from the ground, and in making this very simple observation, the brothers applied their minds to find a means by which this hot air and smoke could somehow be captured and harnessed in order to lift themselves off the ground, to render themselves "weightless." After some near misses with disaster, the Montgolfier brothers finally managed to create a hot air balloon that lifted a sheep, a duck, and a rooster into the air and landed them safely again after several minutes.

Although this was apparently the first time that life-forms had taken to the skies by artificial means, the Montgolfier balloon was not the first use of the hot air balloon; they had been around for quite some time. In fact, as early as 220 CE, the Chinese military used such balloons as unmanned signaling devices in a way not too dissimilar to the way in which Native Americans used smoke signals.

The Montgolfier balloon had been made from linen and paper, and to inflate it the brothers burned straw, chopped wood, and dried manure almost directly under the balloon's opening. The purpose of the manure was to create lots of smoke, which would keep the flames low, thereby preventing the balloon itself from being engulfed in a ball of fire. So, with this innovative thinking, humankind had finally taken to the skies with the thermodynamic lifting power of the hot air balloon. But is it possible that the ancient Egyptians discovered such a technology thousands of years earlier? Could they have harnessed the thermodynamic lifting power of the hot air balloon 4,500 years ago (or longer) and employed it to lift their heavy pyramid blocks?

If the ancient Egyptians could have observed how burning embers from a fire floated upward and wondered what caused this to happen, then it is conceivable that the same thought may have struck them as it did the Montgolfier brothers thousands of years later. And just as the first Montgolfier balloon was made of linen and paper, these just happen to be two materials that were invented by and easily available to the ancient Egyptians, as were ropes, sails, and fire. Egyptian papyrus (an early form of paper made from the pith of the *Cyperus papyrus* plant) was widely used in ancient Egypt and other Mediterranean cultures of the time.

So, the ancient Egyptians certainly could easily have observed the lifting power of hot air, and they certainly had the materials with which they could have created a hot air balloon (or a form of it). But could such a primitive hot air balloon have been able to lift the heavy pyramid blocks?

As previously mentioned, the average weight of a limestone block in the Great Pyramid is often quoted in academic literature as being around 2.5 tons. There are blocks in the Great Pyramid that are much heavier than this (some as much as 70 tons or so), but this figure of 2.5 tons is often quoted as the average block weight. Simple calculations show that a hot air balloon (at sea level) with a diameter of around 125 feet can lift about 6.39 tons, less the weight of the materials used for the balloon itself. Basic calculations using the type of linen material available in the Fourth Dynasty show that a linen balloon of 125 feet diameter would weigh somewhere between 750 and 1,000 pounds. Lifting at night or in the winter months when the air is much cooler would allow better thermodynamic lift than during the day or in the summer months when the ambient temperature would only be slightly less cooler than the air inside the balloon. Of course, the balloon itself would not necessarily have to take the form of a sphere or a bulb, like many modern balloons. Indeed, just about any shape of balloon could work so long as the volume of the balloon envelope was sufficient to capture enough hot air to provide the necessary lift.

Thus we can see that the ancient Egyptians certainly could have observed the lifting power of hot air and that they had the ability and the materials to build hot air balloons, and we can calculate that such a balloon of around 125 feet in diameter, including the weight of the balloon itself and ropes and such, could feasibly lift two average limestone blocks. With the sides of the Great Pyramid being around 750 feet in length, then it would be feasible to have four lifting stations on each face of the pyramid, thus giving, in theory at least, sixteen balloons operating around the pyramid perimeter at any given time, each potentially raising two blocks with each lift. If we assume thirty minutes for each lift then in an eighteen-hour working day, a total of 1,152 stone blocks could theoretically have been raised per day. Although estimates vary, the Great Pyramid is believed to contain somewhere in the region of 2.5 million of these blocks, and as such it would take a little under six years (working every day) to raise this number of stone blocks. This is a little over a third of the time the historian Herodotus quotes for the construction of the Great Pyramid—around twenty years.

But how would the ancient Egyptians have gotten enough hot air into a linen-and-paper balloon to generate the required lift, and how could this have been done without the balloon material itself catching fire and going up in flames? The Montgolfier method of a fire directly under the balloon opening was very precarious and wasn't without its disasters. There may be any number of ways that this could have been achieved, but I will outline here just one method that could have been used and of which there may actually be some physical evidence at the pyramid sites, which will be discussed shortly.

Inflating the balloon with hot air could have been relatively simple through the use of a pair of large, deep stone pits connected near the bottom with a small, horizontal link tunnel; the two pits and the connecting link create a *U* shape. Let's consider how this would work. At the bottom of the first pit a fire is made. Because the fire is in a pit around twenty to thirty feet deep, it is unaffected by the prevailing wind conditions above ground. The small, horizontal link tunnel connecting the first pit to the second pit provides a draft of air that feeds the fire in the first pit, thereby creating a convection current. The real benefit of this type of fire is that it is very efficient and burns very, very hot; is virtually smoke-free; and is entirely controllable. The stone pit being so deep means it is unlikely that the balloon material itself would ever catch fire. Even today small variants of these pit fires are still used around the world and are known as Dakota smokeless fire pits (figure 8.1).

With the fire burning ferociously at the bottom of the left pit (figure 8.1), the opening of the balloon is laid over the mouth of this pit, perhaps with one side of the balloon raised slightly off the ground to allow the fire below to be fed with more fuel as and when required. Very quickly the deflated horizontal balloon will begin to fill with hot air and rise to the vertical. Also, if the balloon material is dyed black then this would help maintain the heat inside the balloon through

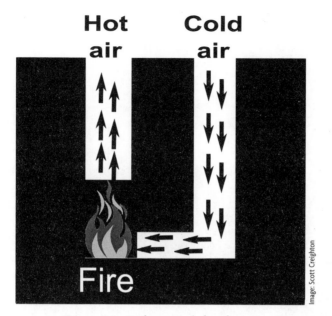

Figure 8.1. Dakota smokeless fire pit

absorption of solar radiation from the hot Egyptian sun, allowing the balloon to remain buoyant longer. Naturally, while being inflated the balloon would have to be anchored to the ground by a rope, just as a modern hot air balloon is.

As the balloon becomes buoyant, a rope net containing the stone blocks is fixed to the fully inflated balloon—the payload. A fixed guy rope that runs from the uppermost level of the pyramid down to the lifting station is looped through a couple of O-rings fitted to the underside of the rope net containing the stone blocks. This will effectively tether the balloon to the guy rope, and when the anchor rope is released, the balloon will float up with its cargo, following the path of the guy rope to the top level of the pyramid (see figure 8.2 on page 192). There may also be a couple of lighter ropes attached to haul the balloon and its "weightless" cargo more quickly up the pyramid slope.

Upon reaching the end of the guy rope at the top of the pyramid, the balloon is once again anchored, and the stones are released from the rope net. The balloon may then be allowed to deflate and recycled

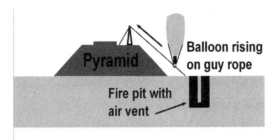

Image: Scott Creighton

Figure 8.2. Hot air balloon carries stone to top of pyramid.

back down the pyramid as another cycle of balloons ascend with their payloads. Or the inflated balloon may be hauled down the pyramid by the other ropes, ready to take up another load. It should be added, of course, that a larger balloon could lift heavier blocks, and by clustering a number of balloons together, even heavier loads might be raised in this manner.

So, through the science of thermodynamics applied to a primitive hot air balloon it may well have been possible for the pyramid stones to have "flown into place"—just as some ancient legends tell us.

PHYSICAL EVIDENCE

But did the ancient Egyptians in fact discover such a lifting technique? Is there any evidence of such? As it turns out, there are some tantalizing clues that hint that they just might have done so. First of all we find that around the perimeter of the pyramids and on the wider Giza plateau there are numerous pits cut deep into the bedrock. These pits

Photos: James Brown

Figure 8.3. Stone pits around Giza with horizontal "air channels" near the base. Note the arrows pointing to connecting air channels.

range from about twenty to as much as sixty feet deep, and some of them are indeed connected by a small horizontal shaft or tunnel near their base (figure 8.3), a tunnel, it should be noted, that is much too small for any person, even a child, to pass through.

This connecting horizontal link tunnel may be the telltale sign for the very type of fire outlined above—the Dakota smokeless fire pit (figure 8.1). As mentioned, one of these deep-hewn stone pits would contain the firewood for burning while the other pit provided a draft of air via the horizontal connecting tunnel to produce the convection current. With the pit hewn directly into the plateau bedrock there would be no possibility of the pit collapsing, and the stone itself within the pit would also heat up, thus boosting the temperature from the pit. And with the fire burning very efficiently in the pit far below the balloon material, burning embers or flames from the fire would be much less likely to set the balloon material ablaze.

A CURIOUS ARTIFACT

Around the Giza plateau several mysterious stone tools in the shape of a mushroom with three curved grooves have been found (figure 8.4). Egyptologists do not really know what this tool was intended for or exactly how it would have been used, but they believe it to be part of some form of proto-pulley system.

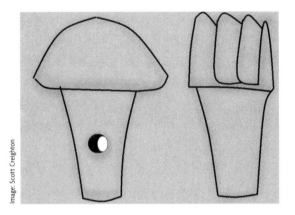

Figure 8.4. Mysterious stone tool found at Giza

Of these strange artifacts, Lehner writes, "The Mystery Tool— Examples of these have been found at Giza, apparently dating to the Old Kingdom. They are mushroom-shaped with one or two holes through the stem and three parallel grooves cut into the head. It has been suggested that they could have been bearing-stones or proto-pulleys, with the stem inserted into a pole or scaffold and the grooves acting as guides for ropes. There is no rimmed wheel, as in a true pulley, but the direction of pull could probably have been changed by running the ropes through the grooves."[2]

This "mystery tool" set into a tall "pole or scaffold" is precisely the kind of tool that would be required at the top level of the pyramid to raise the guy rope sufficiently high enough from the pyramid structure to allow the hot air balloon and its cargo to safely land at the top level of the pyramid (figure 8.5).

The guy rope would pass over the center groove of the mystery

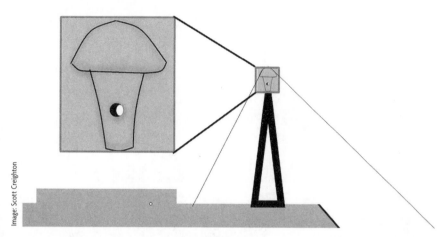

Figure 8.5. Mystery tool fitted to an A-frame to raise and guide the guy rope

tool, whereupon its end would be anchored securely to the pyramid, while the other two grooves could be used as guides for two additional ropes that would be used to haul the balloon and its "weightless" cargo quickly up the pyramid's slope. This tool is not a pulley as such but could merely have functioned as a guide for the ropes to prevent them from rubbing against the sharp edge of the pyramid slope and potentially snagging and snapping.

THE BALLOON BULB

Anyone who has seen a traditional-shaped hot air balloon will recognize its similarity in shape to that of a standard lightbulb. And anyone who has ever attended a hot air balloon flight will have seen how the balloon is first laid flat on the ground; it starts out as a long, thin stretch of material that slowly inflates horizontally on the ground until finally, with sufficient hot air, it gradually rises to the vertical and is ready for takeoff.

In ancient Egyptian art we are often presented with images of flying solar barques, white balloon-like objects surrounded by a pair of wings, suggesting that these balloon-like objects had the ability to take to the sky like a bird. Also, somewhat remarkably, there is even a scene

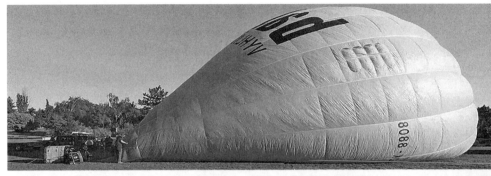

Photo: Roland Ungermigration

Figure 8.6. Top: a horizontal hot air balloon being inflated.
Bottom: relief carving believed by Egyptologists
to show Horus emerging from a lotus flower. But
could that flower instead be a hot air balloon?

in ancient Egyptian art that may depict a hot air balloon actually being inflated. The scene in question (figure 8.6) is presented in the Temple of Hathor at Dendera, and according to conventional Egyptology, it supposedly depicts the ancient Egyptian god Horus emerging from a lotus flower.

Notice how the balloon shape in the lower image in figure 8.6 lies horizontally on its side and is similar to a modern hot air balloon being laid out and filled with hot air, as shown in the upper image. What is also interesting about this particular relief is that the text on the wall alongside it makes mention of the "sky carriers." In some interpretations of this relief the goddess sitting on the stone block to the far right of the image is likely the ancient Egyptian goddess Amaunet, the goddess of air, although this could also be the god Heh, who was also an air/sky god identified with Shu, who supposedly held up the pillars of the sky. Or is Heh referenced in this context, perhaps as holding or carrying someone or something up into the sky? This air goddess is also depicted as a snake (or serpent), which we observe within the center of the balloon-like object.

Intriguingly, on other walls of the Dendera temple are images that also depict this balloon-type object, but in these images the balloons are presented upright (with the snakes of the air goddess Amaunet again depicted within the balloon shape) as though the balloons are now flying up in the air and carrying a cargo in some form of netting or basket beneath them (figure 8.7).

Is it perhaps the case then that in these reliefs we are witnessing a linen balloon being filled with hot air for the lifting of heavy stone blocks? Or does the conventional explanation of this image, that it represents the god Horus being born inside a lotus flower, make more sense? In the context of considering hot air balloons in this image, the depiction of Horus makes perfect sense because this god was, after all, the ancient Egyptian god of the sky.

Objectors to such a proposal will undoubtedly point to the fact that the Temple of Hathor at Dendera was constructed long after the great

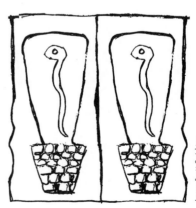

Figure 8.7. Vertical (inflated) balloons depicted in the Dendera temple appear to carry a payload of stones.

Image: Scott Creighton

pyramid-building age. This fact, however, does not invalidate the proposal, because the ancient Egyptians often made reference in their art and texts to practices and rituals whose roots had long since been lost in antiquity and which, in later times, had become couched in the language of religious ritual, the original function and meaning obscured and long lost.

As stated in chapter 7, after the Old Kingdom collapsed, ancient Egypt plunged into a long period of upheaval, chaos, and decline, entering into a relative "dark age" that Egyptologists tell us lasted around two hundred years—long enough for skills and knowledge to be forgotten and lost. Only vague memories would have been passed down to the later generations, campfire stories that would have become legendary, and one of those legendary tales may well have been that the stones of the pyramids "flew into place." If the ancient Egyptians did indeed discover and use the thermodynamic power of the hot air balloon in the manner presented in this chapter, then the legend of the "flying pyramid stones" of ancient Egypt may not be such a "flight of fantasy" as it might at first appear.

9
Project Osiris

The traditional result of Osiris's dismemberment is that there are many so-called tombs of Osiris in Egypt; for Isis held a funeral for each part when she had found it . . . all of them called the tomb of Osiris.

PLUTARCH

The central idea conveyed throughout this book is the idea that the early, giant pyramids of ancient Egypt were built not as tombs to revive ancient Egyptian kings but rather as arks to revive the ancient Egyptian kingdom—the womb of the kingdom rather than the tomb of the king. In the course of the book many new ideas were introduced that sought to explain these pyramids within this controversial alternative paradigm. This chapter will serve to highlight the key aspects of this new theory regarding the ancient Egyptian pyramids.

As stated throughout this book, it is believed by conventional Egyptology that the Egyptian pyramid was the tomb and the instrument that enabled the transfiguration of the dead king into an akh—a glorified being of light that would be effective in the afterlife. In this sense the purpose of the pyramid was to serve as the revivication machine of the king, the device that would ensure his preservation and facilitate his rebirth (revival) in the afterlife. While this religious idea may indeed have been what the ancient Egyptians *eventually* came to believe, we have to ask: Where did such ideas originate? What was it that prompted the ancient Egyptians to develop the religious concept of preservation leading to rebirth?

Even although the evidence of actual human burial in these early pyramids is threadbare in the extreme, it is entirely probable that the very first Egyptian pyramids were later used for the purposes of (intrusive) burials. And it is equally likely that the pyramids of much later dynasties may well have been conceived and constructed as pharaonic tombs and instruments of transfiguration and revivication. This would have been a natural evolution of the ancient Egyptian religious beliefs with regard to the earliest pyramids and their true and original function. It remains my conviction, however, that the first sixteen pyramids built by the ancient Egyptians categorically were *not* conceived or built for the purposes of the entombment or revivication of ancient Egyptian kings, as espoused by Egyptologists, but rather for a much greater and far nobler purpose—as arks to help bring about the revival of the kingdom.

As with most things religious, such ideas and practices—almost without exception—stem from some historical truth or belief, from an actual event having taken place in some remote epoch. In ancient Egypt that event would have had consequences so dire that it would have eventually threatened the very existence of the kingdom, thus it would have been deemed that the best way to ensure that the kingdom could recover from this imminent disaster was to enact a preemptive plan that involved the construction of the first pyramids.

Confronted with such an imminent calamity the ancient Egyptians had little choice. They could do nothing and be certain that their civilization would be lost forever, or they could attempt to preserve *maʾat* (cosmic order), storing the "seeds of rebirth" in massively visible pyramid arks (similar to the primeval mound at the First Time of creation) in the hope that the survivors of their civilization could easily find and breach them to make use of their life-sustaining contents. In so doing, the ancient Egyptians could maintain ma'at by safeguarding the means by which the kingdom could be revived.

And the ancient Egyptians understood, probably better than most, the cycle of life, death, and rebirth. They observed in the rising and setting sun, the rising and setting stars, and the waxing and waning of the moon the recurrent cycles of death and rebirth. The great River Nile, the lifeblood of their civilization, ebbed and flowed; their pharaohs lived, died, and were believed to be reborn among the stars in the afterlife.

Everything in the ancient Egyptians' worldview had its own cycle of life, death, and rebirth. What is often overlooked, however, is their belief that just like the sun, the moon, the planets, the stars, and their kings, the *Earth* itself also followed a cycle of life, death, and rebirth. And this cycle of the Earth is not the simple annual passing of the seasons but something much more profound: a cycle of death and rebirth of the kind that had occurred at the First Time (Zep Tepi) of creation when chaos ensued and when the Earth—in the form of the primeval mound—first arose from the primordial flood waters. As Plato wrote in his *Timaeus,* "Whereas just when you and other nations are beginning to be provided with letters and the other requisites of civilized life, after the usual interval, the stream from heaven, like a pestilence, comes pouring down and leaves only those of you who are destitute of letters and education, and so you have to begin all over again like children and know nothing of what happened in ancient times, either among us or among yourselves."[1]

This cycle of death and rebirth is the underlying concept that permeates through all aspects of ancient Egyptian religious thought. While Egyptologists will debate endlessly as to whether the ancient Egyptian religion was primarily stellar or solar in nature (or both), it is my belief that the overarching religious belief—the *core* belief—of the ancient Egyptians fundamentally concerned itself with cycles of death and rebirth, or rather, of creation, death, and revivication. But more than that, it was about meticulous, preemptive planning before death to ensure revivication and, ultimately, to preserve the cosmic order of ma'at.

This the ancient Egyptians sought to do by building temples to their various gods, and within those temples they would make offerings and recite prayers to the various deities they believed powered all elements essential for the maintenance of the cosmic order. They did everything in their power to ensure that revivication could occur at the end of each of the various cosmic cycles, including the revivication of the Earth from a global flood they believed would one day bring about its death, a death they believed had been shown to them in the stars. To the ancient Egyptians this imminent "death" of the Earth—of their civilization—was more than just a belief; it was the word of Thoth himself, one of their oldest and wisest gods.

Egyptologists explain the absence of any contemporary royal mummies having ever been recovered from any of the pre–Fifth Dynasty pyramids as the work of tomb robbers. At the same time, however, they are somewhat befuddled by the large amounts of wheat, barley, grape, and other types of seeds found in a number of galleries under the Step Pyramid of Djoser, as well as in other underground silos around this pyramid complex. They are further unable to easily explain the massive cache of forty thousand vases, plates, pots, and other artifacts also found under this pyramid.

Certainly in much later tombs such as that of Tutankhamun, pots, plates, vases, seeds, and various other artifacts have been found and are believed to be for use in the king's afterlife. But generally, the artifacts in these much later underground tombs are always of small, symbolic amounts—a few pots and vases, a handful of seeds. This is in no way comparable with the tens of thousands of vessels and massive amounts of seed that were recovered from under Djoser's pyramid complex, which are far in excess of what one would expect for symbolic needs. Of course, most other chambers in Djoser's pyramid (and in all pyramids) would have been picked clean of such recovery goods—as was the intention. However, that such a large cache was found mostly intact is exceedingly fortunate for it allows us to glimpse the true picture and purpose of these structures as arks—the means to effect the revivication of the kingdom at the time of its "death by deluge."

Based on the belief in these cycles of creation followed by death, the ancient Egyptians ensured that everything was done, everything was prepared and set in its proper place beforehand in order that the desired revivication could come about for the Earth to be revived. Without these proactive and preemptive measures put in place, the revivication of the Earth could never occur and its death would be permanent. A fine example of this religious thought is exemplified by the great sun temples built all over Egypt by the later ancient Egyptians. In these great sun temples the priests would chant and recite their prayers to the sun god, counting the hours of the night, praying that their spells and incantations would appease the gods and bring forth the sun, revived and rejuvenated once again on the eastern horizon—the place of rebirth.

Revivication—this is the central theme, the driving force that underpinned all ancient Egyptian religious thought and one that would ultimately inspire the construction of the largest monuments on Earth, monuments so great that they could forever ensure the revival, the re-creation of the Earth (i.e., the Egyptian civilization) at the appointed time of its "death" from a massive deluge and devastating drought.

THE BODY OF OSIRIS

The early, giant pyramids of ancient Egypt at Abu Roash, Saqqara, Dahshur, Meidum, and Giza are, without doubt, the most enigmatic and enduring man-made structures ever built. As stated throughout this book, we are told by conventional thought that these pyramids were built by a succession of Third and Fourth Dynasty kings to serve as their eternal tomb and instrument of revivication. We are further told that there was no grand plan involved in setting down any of these pyramids, that each of the kings in whose names these structures were supposedly constructed cared little for what pyramids went before or may have come after their own. Each ancient Egyptian king is believed to have built his pyramid to his own personal taste and without knowledge of or reference to any master plan. Egyptian kings, it is said, did not plan or build tombs for their successor or their successor's successor.

However, in the ancient Egyptians' earliest religious writings, the Pyramid Texts, we are told that the "pyramid is Osiris" and "this construction is Osiris." In Plutarch's *Isis and Osiris* we are further told that the body of Osiris had been cut into sixteen (or fourteen) pieces. As I stated in chapter 2, it is not unreasonable to propose that these sixteen dismembered parts of Osiris were in fact an allegorical reference to the first sixteen pyramids completed by the ancient Egyptians and that, in time, these sixteen pyramids became the metaphorical body of Osiris, just like Christian churches today are referred to as the body of Christ. These sixteen pyramid arks, packed full with all manner of recovery items, were the proactive and preemptive means by which the ancient Egyptians hoped the Earth (their kingdom) could be revived and re-created after its "death."

As arks the pyramids would have contained, among many other things, vast quantities of various seed types such as wheat, barley, grape, and others—the sixteen-piece pyramid body of Osiris packed with seeds. And we note, also as mentioned in chapter 2, that in later dynasties the ancient Egyptians would fashion small effigies of Osiris from mud. These were known as corn mummies because the ancient Egyptians would then pack this miniature body of Osiris with various seeds. This ritual was part of the Osiris rebirth Festival of Khoiak.

Associated with these corn mummies was the Osiris brick or Osiris bed. These were small hollowed-out wooden boxes or stone-fired containers that resembled a minisarcophagus, or *nebankh*. Within these small containers the ancient Egyptians would place some earth, sprinkle it with seed in the shape of Osiris, and then bury it in the ground under a large boulder, thereby symbolizing the original nebankh (Osiris bed) that had been placed within the pyramid to hold the life force, or ka, of Osiris within the pyramid body of Osiris.

The growing seed within the Osiris beds symbolized the rebirth of the kingdom (the Earth) through the agency and regenerative power of Osiris. This particular ritual at the Festival of Khoiak was likely in remembrance of the original Osiris bed.

When the Italian pyramid explorer Giovanni Belzoni first entered the second pyramid at Giza (G2) in 1818, he found earth and bones within a granite container, a discovery that Belzoni initially believed to have been human remains, possibly belonging to Khafre. But when these bones were sent to the naturalist William Clift at the Royal College of Surgeons' Hunterian Museum in London, it was discovered that these remains were not human at all but were in fact the bones of a *bull*—the ba of Osiris. In Egyptian hieroglyphs the bull is associated with the soul, thus these stone containers symbolically held the soul of Osiris within the pyramid body of Osiris.

Conventional Egyptology writes off the discovery of earth and bull bones in the so-called sarcophagus of G2 as an intrusive burial or as an offering to the gods. In the words of Belzoni:

> A young man of the name of Pieri, employed in the counting house of Briggs and Walmas in Cairo, came the next day to visit the pyramid, and, having rummaged the rubbish inside of the sarcophagus, found a piece of bone, which we supposed to belong to a human skeleton. On searching farther, we found several pieces, which, having been sent to London, proved to be the bones of a bull.
>
> Some consequential persons, however, who would not scruple to sacrifice a point in history, rather than lose a *bon mot*, thought themselves mighty clever in baptizing the said bones those of a cow, merely to raise a joke. So much for their taste for antiquity.[2]

But not everyone of Belzoni's time shared his view, as this 1822 extract from *The Gentleman's Magazine and Historical Chronicle* shows.

Signior Belzoni has returned to England, and has published his Travels, operations, and astonishing discoveries in Egypt and Nubia. Mr. Faber expressed a decided opinion that the sarcophagi of the pyramids were intended solely to deposit the remains of the sacred bull, contrary to the testimonies of Herodotus, Diodorus Siculus, and other ancient historians. The bones of a bull have indeed been found by Belzoni in the pyramid of Cepherenes, and in the great tomb of the valley Beban el Malook; yet this enterprising and indefatigable traveler takes the liberty of differing from the opinion of the Rev. Mr. Faber, and declares his conviction that these stupendous structures "were erected as Sepulchers," and that the Pyramid in question undoubtedly contained the remains of "some great personage. . . ." But why should Mr. Faber so sarcastically express his surprise . . . why feel himself provoked at this discovery of the bull's bones, unaccompanied by those of the sovereign? The event proves, that the religion, or rather their infatuating idolatry, was more potent than their preservation of its object. Diodorus has told us . . . that Cepherenes, by his conduct, had rendered himself odious to the people, and that they threatened to disturb his remains. They are not found in the pyramid!! As to the sepulchral honors conferred on the sacred bull, the same historian, Diodorus . . . after describing the religious ceremonies in their worship of Isis and Osiris, noticing the traditionary mandates of the former to the priests of Egypt with regard to the adoration of Osiris, writes as follows. . . .

"To honor Osiris as a god, to consecrate whatever animal they may choose, bred in the country—to worship it while alive in like manner as they formerly did Osiris, and after its death to confer similar funeral honors."

Thus the rolls of antiquity announce the most solemn, splendid burial of the bull or Apis, and the cow or Isis; and after the lapse of thousands of years, the tombs which at the time of this worship were carefully concealed from the public eye, are penetrated at length by the travelers of the present day; the sacred relics, which they have just discovered, are accordingly found to be accompanied with all the pomp imaginable and are ocular and additional evidence of historic veracity. That the pyramids may also have been originally intended to commemorate the Flood, appears extremely probable: it is an opinion long ago entertained, and lately supported by Mr. Faber, with acknowledged erudition. But this did not preclude the occasional appropriation of these structures as tombs for their Kings.[3]

Egyptology essentially concurs with Belzoni's view that these bull bones represent a much later, intrusive burial (perhaps relating to some ritual after the king's body had been removed) and does not actually consider the possibility that Belzoni's discovery of earth and bull bones within the granite container of G2 might actually have been its *original* content, that these containers of earth and bull bones symbolically represented the soul of Osiris (within the pyramid body of Osiris). As Lehner states, "Curiously, bones found in the sarcophagus turned out to be those of a bull. In a much later period bulls were buried as symbols of the pharaoh himself or of Osiris. Rainer Stadelmann has suggested that these bones were probably an offering thrown into the sarcophagus at some unknown later date by intruders, long after the king's body had been robbed and lost."[4]

Given the clear tradition in ancient Egypt of intrusive burials, we have to ask why it would make more sense to give over a supposedly empty sarcophagus for the "burial" of earth and the bones of a bull? And why, we might ask, wasn't a surrogate ka statue of the original missing king placed inside the empty sarcophagus, thereby ensuring his continued place in the afterlife? And furthermore, if it had been discovered that the ancient remains of Khafre had been robbed, then this would have provided the reigning king or pharaoh the perfect opportunity to appropriate Khafre's pyramid for his own intrusive, royal burial. But no—we are to believe that the reigning king turned down such a golden opportunity to safeguard his afterlife and glorify himself for all eternity, and instead went to the not inconsiderable trouble of filling the granite box in Khafre's pyramid with nothing but earth and the bones of a bull. Something here simply doesn't add up.

Clearly, the tracking down and dating of these bones might help provide a more definitive answer as to their provenance and purpose. To this end I contacted the acting curator of the Royal College of Surgeons in London to ask what had become of Belzoni's bull bones. Alas, it seems that the bull bones from this stone container have become lost, as explained to me in a private e-mail.

> William Clift was the first curator of the museum upon its opening in 1813 and acquired a large amount of material which was added to the collections. Unfortunately, the college was badly bombed during World War Two and we lost over two thirds of our collections. I'm sorry to say it appears as though this specimen may have been one of the destroyed items as we now have no record of its whereabouts. There is a chance that it may have been one of the rare survivors that was de-accessioned due to the destruction of the college building and transferred across to the Natural History Museum.[5]

Having subsequently contacted the Natural History Museum in London, I was somewhat disappointed to learn that they did not have this specimen in their collection either, so, it would seem, that Belzoni's bull bones may be lost forever.

But the fact of the matter remains that this curious discovery within the stone container of G2 should not at all be considered peculiar, and, as explained above, it is perfectly explainable within the cultural ideas and religious practices of the ancient Egyptians; there is a cultural context for an earth-filled stone container to have been placed within the early, giant pyramids. With this earth-filled container in the pyramid of Khafre we have a direct link between this original container and the later practice of burying small, replica containers (Osiris bricks) filled with earth under a "mound of creation" (generally a large boulder). It was a chthonic ritual celebrating the pyramids as the revivication instruments of the Earth, laid out along the banks of the Nile in the form of Osiris, a stone container to hold the ka and ba (i.e., the soul of Osiris) within the sixteen-part pyramid body of Osiris.

A small number of Osiris beds have been found in Egyptian tombs, most notably that of Tutankhamun. These artifacts symbolized the chthonic reemergence of life, and it is possible that their use goes far back into antiquity, possibly even *before* the pyramid-building age.

Of Osiris bricks and Osiris beds, Egyptologist Angela Tooley writes:

Osiris Bricks. . . . These are related to the Festival of Khoiak when images of Osiris were made of soil and grain. The containers are defined as matrices for the creation of such Osiris figures. . . .

Osiris bricks are little known. They appear most frequently in exhibition catalogues, with little discussion. Typically they are of fired red pottery, are rectangular in shape and resemble ordinary bricks, on average 24cm long, 12cm wide and 6cm deep. Although they are remarkably consistent in shape and dimensions, all the bricks are individual and handmade. Roughly half of the known bricks have a shallow rebate in the upper face, probably to accommodate a lid, while the remaining examples are flat-topped.

Recessed centrally or off-center into the upper face of each brick is an image of Osiris between 18 and 25 cm long and 2 to 4 cm in depth. He is shown in profile, wearing the *atef*-crown and long ceremonial beard, and carrying a crook and flail. . . .

Charles Lortet worked in the Wadi Qubbanet el Qi-rud in 1905, finding not only corn-mummies but also other types of Osiris figures. In 1916 Howard Carter rediscovered the wadi, noting that the wadi mouth contained "mimic" burials comprising mummiform figures in faience, wood and stone in pottery coffins, as well as many corn-mummies placed below large boulders.[6]

What we actually have here then is a cultural explanation for the earth and bull bones found in the stone container within G2—the nebankh or "possessor of life," the stone container that possessed the invisible life force or "vital spark" of the ka. Conversely, we are also presented with a cultural explanation for the mummyless stone containers found in the pyramids and the reason why, as mentioned in chapter 3, not a single one of these containers in any of these pyramids (unlike mastaba sarcophagi of this period) was ever inscribed with any names or titles of any ancient Egyptian king when, in terms of the religious beliefs of the time, such might have been expected.

In short, the stone containers found within the early, giant pyramids may not have been sarcophagi for a dead king at all but rather might have served as an integral part of a deep, chthonic ritual relating to the revivication of the Earth through the agency of Osiris. They might be a link to a stone container filled with earth that symbolized the life force or ka of Osiris, an earth-filled stone container that was actually found by Belzoni in G2 (the archetype of the Osiris brick and Osiris bed), and the nebankh that would appear in smaller, symbolic forms in later times during the festival celebrating the rebirth of Osiris.

For conventional Egyptology to continue to insist that the earth and bull bones discovered by Belzoni in the stone container of G2 were nothing more than a later intrusive burial serves only to misinform and mislead; it's a ploy designed solely to prop up and perpetuate a flawed paradigm (i.e., the pyramid tomb theory). This crucial piece of evidence and the misguided interpretation Egyptology has applied to it represents perhaps one of the pivotal moments where conventional Egyptology may have taken a fundamental wrong turn in formulating its ideas about the function of the first pyramids. Ever since Belzoni's erroneous assumption, his complete failure to recognize that there was another cultural narrative to explain the earth-filled stone container he had found, every Egyptologist who followed in his wake has been hammering the same square peg into the same round hole.

In failing to make this simple connection between the earth in the nebankh of Khafre's Pyramid and the earth in the later Osiris bricks and corn mummies (i.e., miniature nebankhs or "containers of life"), this would become the first of many wrong turns Egyptologists would make with regard to the understanding of the early, giant pyramids and why they struggle—even to this day—to reconcile their pyramid tomb theory and its missing mummies with the actual evidence. In short, regarding the discovery by Belzoni in the sarcophagus of G2, Egyptologists have had to concoct a truly bizarre scenario in order to explain this contradictory evidence and to shoehorn the pyramid tomb theory into their preconceived notions. But, as repeatedly stated, there is every possibility that the material found in 1818 by Belzoni in the stone container of G2 actually represented its *original* contents and that these granite boxes in these first pyramids may in fact have been the archetype of the later tradition of the Osiris bricks and beds and the corn mummies. And if this is so—and there is little reason to doubt it—then it places a monumental question mark over the veracity and legitimacy of the preferred tomb theory that Egyptology has been advocating for the best part of two hundred years.

RAISING THE DJED PILLAR

The Osirian Festival of Khoiak would culminate with a ceremony known as raising the djed pillar. The djed pillar (figure 9.1) was also closely associated with the god Osiris and is generally regarded as symbolizing his backbone. Thus the raising of the djed pillar is essentially raising Osiris, who is set on his side (i.e., dead) so that when the pillar is raised, he becomes upright (i.e., revived). Other interpretations of this ceremony assert that the djed pillar represents the lost phallus of Osiris and that the raising of the djed pillar actually represents the phallus being made erect, thus it is a potent symbol of the regenerative power

Image: Jeff Dahl

Figure 9.1. Djed pillar

and fecundity of Osiris. As Budge wrote in *The Book of the Dead,* "Sailing about she gathered the fragments of Osiris's body. Wherever she found one, there she built a tomb. . . . By the festival celebrated by the Egyptians in honor of the model of the lost member of Osiris, we are probably to understand the public performance of the ceremony of 'setting up the Tet in Tattu' [Djed Pillar], which we know took place on the last day of the month Choiak."[7]

But the pyramid arks represented but *one* aspect of Project Osiris; they were the physical hardware, the practical storage facilities. For the revivication of the Earth to be "guaranteed," then the gods would have had to be appeased just as they had to be appeased in their sun temples to ensure the sun would be reborn each and every day. And so, much like the sun temples, Project Osiris ensured that the pyramid arks would also be equipped with chthonic temples built on their eastern flanks (east being the place of rebirth), in which the priests could recite their prayers and spells that would ensure the Earth, just like the sun, could be revived and rejuvenated after its coming "death." And it may even have been that the ancient Egyptians went so far as to depict the desired revivication of the Earth by inscribing all manner of plants, animals, and heavenly bodies—everything in creation— onto the walls of the great causeways that connected the two chthonic temples in a great burst of energy, of creation, shooting forth from the eastern face of the pyramid, everything pouring out of the pyramid in a great burst of life to revive the Earth—just as the primeval mound had done at the First Time of creation when it arose from the primordial flood waters.

In this sense it is easy to understand how the pyramids and their associated chthonic temples, having been the great body of Osiris that ensured the revivication of a dying kingdom, would have become revered by later dynasties and how the pyramid itself (and its function as a repository of seeds and other vital recovery items) would naturally have evolved into a religious icon. As such, it is easy to understand how this would—in time—have further evolved into a religion that practiced the corporeal preservation and rebirth of the king himself, with Osiris now a god and placed at the very heart of what had become a revivication ritual of the king himself. In this regard, Egyptologist John G. Griffiths writes:

> There was something different in the Osirian conception of immortality. First, it was a corporeal conception. Whereas the other religious systems involved the ascent of the deceased to heaven or his temporary transformation into another form, the Osirian system is clearly concerned with the body of the dead king and desiderates continued life for his body. Death indeed is not usually admitted. As Osiris, the tired god, was able to revive from his sleep, so the king will awake and stand. . . . Death is really only a sleep, then, a phase of tiredness; and the firm denial of it in other references shows that it is denied both as a state and as an occurrence.
>
> "O king, thou hast not gone away dead; though hast gone away alive. Sit on the throne of Osiris." (Pyramid Texts 134a–b)
>
> Here then is a doctrine of continued life rather than of resurrection or resuscitation after death. In view of the pretence or euphemism involved one should possibly not object to the common use

of the term resurrection as a description of the doctrine, although it is not precisely correct; it is the non-Osirian doctrine, in various forms, which amounts to a belief in resurrection.[8]

This "Osirian doctrine" as it pertains to the religious rites of the king was unlike earlier Egyptian religious thought; it proposed a wholly corporeal revivication (from sleep) in the *present plane* of existence rather than a spiritual or metaphysical rebirth in the netherworld. And so, in terms of the pyramids as arks that held within them the means to revive a devastated (injured but not dead) kingdom, it is easy to understand how this Osirian doctrine correlates with such an idea and how the corporeal nature of the Osirian doctrine would, in time, come to influence ancient Egyptian religious thought so profoundly.

This is to say that through the agency of Osiris (i.e., the sixteen-part pyramid arks), the kingdom would have the means to rise again and would do so in *this* physical realm. The ancient Egyptians did not imagine the revival of their kingdom as some spiritual occurrence; it was to happen in the corporeal world of the future through meticulous contingency planning by physically storing everything that would be needed to revive the kingdom within massive, physical, pyramid arks. And this concept of the kingdom "sleeping" (after the deluge) and being "revived" in *this* physical realm would become a religious idea that would, in time, be transferred to the king himself; the king would now *also* have a fully corporeal rebirth in *this* realm, provided, of course, he was supplied with all the necessary "equipment" to facilitate his revival.

With all their preparations made and having set everything in place to ensure the Earth's recovery (i.e., its revivication), the ancient Egyptians knew it was now only a matter of time before the gods would bring the kingdom to its knees. And it is a matter of historical fact that the Old Kingdom—whose people built the first, giant pyramids—suddenly collapsed along with most other early Bronze Age cultures. As shown in chapter 7, considerable evidence has come to light in recent years to indicate that the cause of this sudden collapse was a severe drought brought about by sudden and catastrophic climate change whereby many of the cultures at that time—including the Akkadian Empire—simply disappeared from history. Ancient Egypt, however, like a phoenix, was somehow able to rise from the ashes of its demise and rebuild itself. It is my opinion that ancient Egypt was able to do this because, unlike other cultures of the time, ancient Egypt, by planning and implementing a national disaster-recovery system (Project Osiris—the great pyramid arks and their associated chthonic temples), had put in place the means to secure its own preservation and corporeal revival. It is little surprise then that one of the most sacred symbols in ancient Egypt, the pyramid-shaped benben stone, is associated with the *bennu* bird, a bird that is said to possess the same rebirth qualities as the phoenix.

It is also perfectly understandable, in this context, that the chthonic god Osiris came to be regarded by later dynasties as the god of agriculture and of rebirth and regeneration, because this is precisely what the early, giant pyramid arks (the body of Osiris) actually did; these mounds of creation, this Project Osiris, safeguarded the revival of the ancient Egyptian civilization into a new age.

10

Journey's End

I always looked for excavations, for the secrets under the sand.

ZAHI HAWASS[1]

Time was running out. It was a little after 8:00 a.m., and I was sched-
uled to depart Egypt at 4:00 p.m. that afternoon, and still I had not
been able to achieve my goal. Squatting on the floor of my hotel room,
surrounded by all manner of maps of Giza and Cairo, I tried to find
an alternative route to the apex point to the southwest of the plateau. For certain the direct approach crossing the Giza plateau itself
was simply not possible, with Zahi's Wall and the guards patrolling it
being something of an insurmountable obstacle. I would have to cir-
cumvent the plateau and approach the apex location from the opposite
direction in the south. My close brush with the Egyptian authorities the previous day remained all too vivid in my mind, a reminder,
should I have needed it, of just how difficult my task would be. I had
managed to talk my way out of trouble on that occasion but knew
that you can only push your luck so far; next time I might not be so
fortunate.

But I had come so far and had literally been within a few hundred yards of my goal, the apex point, only to be thwarted at the very last moment. Lying on the floor beside me was my small granite pyramid, my little gift to Osiris. Looking at it now brought mixed feelings of failure but also of resolve. I glanced at the table clock. There was time enough yet, and I felt I had to give it one more try for I did not know how long it would be before I could visit Egypt again.

So, once more, time was of the essence. Having ensured that all my belongings had been packed and left with the concierge (I had to be back to the hotel by 2:00 p.m. at the latest), I set off from my hotel around 9:00 a.m., my resolve gaining new impetus with the added time constraint.

Again it was a very typical Egyptian day—blue skies, hot sunshine, and a cacophony of noise. There would be no taxi this time. My plan was to walk alongside the perimeter of the plateau, heading south until I was in line with the apex location, and hope that I would find some opening in the perimeter security fence around that location.

Once again it would be a long and uncomfortable walk—several kilometers in the blazing sunshine. But at least this time by following the main road south, I would not feel so alone, with the occasional local Egyptian passing by, going about his or her everyday life. After about an hour following the perimeter security fence of the plateau, I was beginning to get the distinct impression that it was never going to end; it just kept going and going and going. This wasn't looking promising. Beyond the perimeter fence I could now see a part of the wall with manned security watchtowers stretching across the sand dunes (see figure 10.1 on page 218). It seemed that the Egyptians authorities certainly took the security of the plateau very seriously indeed.

But I persevered. I knew that I could only walk on for about another hour, whereupon I would have no option but to turn around to make the two-hour walk back to my hotel, have a quick shower, and head for the airport. As each minute ticked passed and there was little sign of

Photos: Scott Creighton

Figure 10.1. Security walls, fences, and towers around Giza

any clear opening in the security fence, I grew increasingly anxious. I just kept walking and looking, catching fleeting glimpses of the pyramids in the distance beyond great dunes of sand.

Soon I had reached my point of no return. Two hours and several kilometers had now passed, and still there was no gap to be found in the perimeter fence. I reckoned by now I was probably almost in line with the apex location, which would have been almost exactly due east of where I was standing; if only I could get myself inside the security fence, I would have been able to walk to my destination in a matter of about five minutes or so.

But there was simply no opening to be found anywhere; this fence just went on and on for as far as the eye could see. But I walked on for about a minute more and, amazingly, came across a gate. My heart leaped with joy—only to be instantly crushed when I noticed the heavy chain and padlock that were securing it tightly shut.

Inside the security fence, about twenty yards beyond the security gate, I could see three local Egyptian men digging up a road. Things were becoming desperate now, and time was a commodity that had essentially run out. I thought that perhaps the men had a key to the gate and, with the help of some baksheesh, might be persuaded to open it and allow me entry. I tentatively called out to them. At first they ignored my calls, but as I persisted, one of them eventually came over.

I could barely speak a word of Arabic, so the only thing I could think of was to take out my small granite pyramid. When the man arrived I showed him the granite stone and pointed to the hill beyond where he was working. He smiled at me and shrugged his shoulders. He had no idea what I was meaning. Why would he? I grabbed a handful of dollars from my pocket and took hold of the chain and lock, shaking them and displaying the dollars. He seemed to get the message and kept smiling at me. He could either open the gate—or not. After some anxious moments of deliberation, he simply turned around and walked back to join his colleagues, leaving me utterly crushed and deflated.

Once again I was probably less than a few hundred yards from my destination, and once again I had been thwarted with security fences. It seemed peculiarly ironic that only a few days before I had stood in the Sphinx enclosure, one of the most secure and difficult-to-access sites in all Egypt, yet I could not find access to a barren, unremarkable part of the Egyptian desert. I stood for a minute or so simply gaping through the locked gate at the small hill in the distance—my goal. I looked down at my gift to Osiris—so near and yet so far. Disappointed and dejected, I returned the small pyramid stone to my backpack and, with a heavy heart, about-turned on the road, headed back to my hotel, to the airport, and home to Scotland.

Upon returning home I wrote about my experience on my Abovetopsecret.com web forum. I also wrote to Hawass, explaining the centroid theory and how the three pyramids "pointed" to a specific location to the southwest of the plateau and that this might be an area of interest worth excavating. You can imagine my surprise when—only months after making this possible location public—this precise area of the Egyptian desert (an unremarkable area that had remained undisturbed probably since Egypt was formed millions of years ago) was now the site of a major excavation (see figures 10.2a–d on pages 220–21).

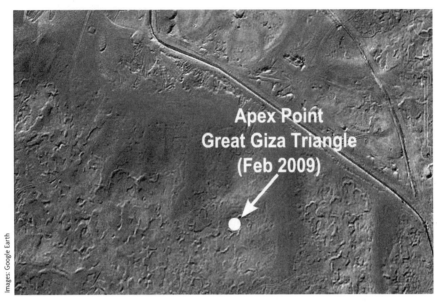

Figure 10.2a. *The undisturbed Apex location of the Great Giza Triangle as of February 2009, before excavation begins.*

Figure 10.2b. *Excavation of the Apex location begins in March 2009.*

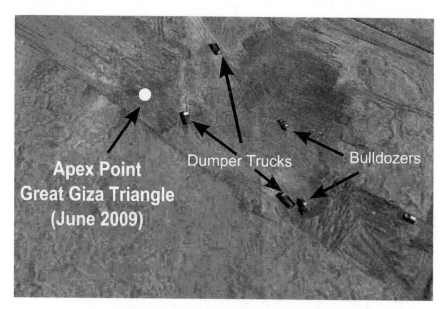

Figure 10.2c. Excavation around the Apex Point continues in June 2009.

Figure 10.2d. Excavation around the Apex Point is completed, June 2009.

Having learned of this major excavation activity at the very location of the apex point, I wrote to Hawass and asked if he knew the purpose of this digging. He did not reply. A short time after posting the images in figure 10.2 on the Official Graham Hancock Website (www.grahamhancock.com), a poster there, Dennis Payne, sent me some gamma-filtered images of the apex location, pointing out some underground features that appear fairly geometric in shape, like underground chambers of some kind (figure 10.3a–b).

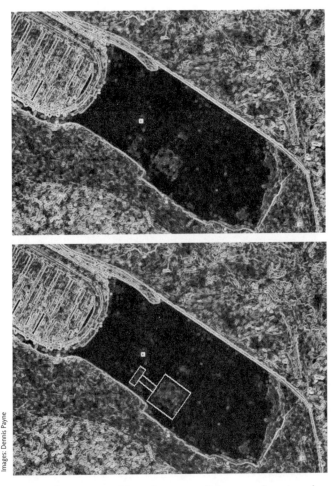

Figure 10.3a–b. Gamma-filtered images of the apex location show what appears to be a geometric formation beneath the surface.

What might the purpose of such intensive excavating in this area have been? Is it but a mere coincidence that this area was majorly excavated only months after I had made Hawass aware of this location and had also published that information on Abovetopsecret.com and Graham Hancock's website, explaining why this area might be of great historical significance? Might this area really be the secret location of the legendary Chamber of Osiris? And might the Egyptian authorities have discovered the lost ark of the gods, the missing part of the "body" of Osiris?

Perhaps only time will tell.

HYMN TO OSIRIS

"Homage to thee, Osiris, Lord of eternity, King of the Gods, whose names are manifold, whose forms are holy, thou being of hidden form in the temples, whose Ka is holy. . . . Thou makest thy soul to be raised up. Thou art the Lord of the Great House in Khemenu. . . . Thy name is established in the mouths of men. Thou art the substance of Two Lands. Thou art Tem, the feeder of Kau, the Governor of the Companies of the gods. Thou art the beneficent Spirit among the spirits. The god of the Celestial Ocean draweth from thee his waters. Thou sendest forth the north wind at eventide, and breath from thy nostrils to the satisfaction of thy heart. Thy heart reneweth its youth. . . . The stars in the celestial heights are obedient unto thee, and the great doors of the sky open themselves before thee. Thou art he to whom praises are ascribed in the southern heaven, and thanks are given for thee in the northern heaven. The imperishable stars are under thy supervision, and the stars which never set are thy thrones."[2]

Notes

FOREWORD

1. Honore, *Slow Fix,* epigraph.
2. Ibid., 280.

CHAPTER 1. LEGENDS OF SECRET CHAMBERS

1. Lepre, *Egyptian Pyramids,* 65.
2. Petrie, *Pyramids and Temples,* 421.
3. Higgins, *Ancient Freemasonry,* 105.
4. Cayce, *Edgar Casey's Egypt,* 207.
5. Joseph Robert Jochmans, "1995: The Hall of Records: Will the Legendary Egyptian Treasure Trove Be Rediscovered?" www.think-aboutit .com/1995-hall-records (accessed June 2, 2014).
6. Murtadi, *Egyptian History.*
7. Lehner, *Complete Pyramids,* 40–41.
8. Gary Osborn, "Re: IT'S TIME," Mysteries message board at the Official Graham Hancock Website, April 20, 2012, 6:45 p.m., www .grahamhancock.com/phorum/read.php?f=1&i=312995&t=312274# reply_312995 (accessed May 30, 2014).
9. Budge, *Fetish to God,* 198.
10. Joseph Robert Jochmans, "1995: The Hall of Records: Will the Legendary Egyptian Treasure Trove Be Rediscovered?" www.think -aboutit.com/1995-hall-records (accessed July 7, 2014).

11. Massey, *Gerald Massey's Lectures,* 7.

12. Picknett and Prince, *Sion Revelation,* 383–84.

CHAPTER 2. IN THE FOOTSTEPS OF THE ANCIENTS

1. Doreal, *Emerald Tablets,* 378.

2. Pyramid Texts, 1657.

3. Plutarch, *Isis and Osiris,* vol. 5, *Moralia,* 45.

CHAPTER 3. A WRONG TURN

1. Zivie-Coche, *Sphinx,* 102.

2. Lepre, *Egyptian Pyramids,* 268.

3. "Kawab," Wikipedia, http://en.wikipedia.org/wiki/Kawab (accessed August 8, 2014).

4. Ibid.

5. "Meresankh II," Wikipedia, http://en.wikipedia.org/wiki/Meresankh_II (accessed August 8, 2014).

6. "Minkhaf I," Wikipedia, http://en.wikipedia.org/wiki/Minkhaf_I (accessed August 8, 2014).

7. Brian Alm, "Ancient Egyptian Religion, Part 7—Roots Too Deep to Dislodge," Egyptological, August 2012, http://egyptological.com/2012/08/14/ancient-egyptian-religion-part-7-roots-too-deep-to-dislodge-9777 (accessed May 30, 2014).

8. Lehner, *Complete Pyramids,* 134.

9. Smyth, *Our Inheritance in the Great Pyramid,* 358.

10. Philip A. Femano, "The Granite Plugs of the Great Pyramid," Egyptological, September 2011, http://egyptological.com/2011/09/09/the-granite-plugs-of-the-great-pyramid-5415 (accessed May 30, 2014).

CHAPTER 4. BARRIERS TO DISCOVERY

1. Mohamed Al Fayed, "Tartan's Egyptian Connections," www.alfayed.com/news-and-opinion/copy-of-christmas-parade-2009.aspx.

2. Evans, *Kingdom of the Ark,* 280.

3. Zahi Hawass, private communication with Scott Creighton.

4. "Pyramid Revamp Fences Out Hawkers," BBC News, August 12, 2008, http://news.bbc.co.uk/1/hi/world/middle_east/7556225.stm (accessed May 30, 2014).

CHAPTER 5. THOTH: HARBINGER OF THE DELUGE

1. Budge, *Legends of the Gods,* xxxi–xxxii.
2. Budge, *From Fetish to God,* 198.
3. Assmann, *Mind of Egypt,* 58.
4. Naydler, *Temple of the Cosmos,* 207.
5. Lehner, *Complete Pyramids,* 24.
6. Strouhal, *Life of the Ancient Egyptians,* 92.
7. BBC, "Sacred Ibis," www.biologydir.com/sacred-ibis-threskiornis-aethiopicus-info-11882.html (accessed July 7, 2014).
8. Schoedler, *Book of Nature,* 580.
9. Allen, *Ancient Egyptian Pyramid Texts,* 33.

CHAPTER 6. GUNPOWDER AND PLOT

1. *Journals of the House of Commons,* Vol. 62, 680.
2. Vyse, *Operations,* Vol. I, 225.
3. Edwards, *The Pyramids of Egypt,* 141.
4. Sitchin, *Journeys,* 30–31.
5. Vyse, *Operations,* Vol. I, 216.
6. Vyse, Private Journal, entry from June 16th, 1837.
7. Ibid., entry from May 27th, 1837.
8. Dina Abdel-Alim, Day 7 Magazine, www.youm7.com/News.asp?NewsID=1356323#.U7vtrUCdTfX (accessed July 8, 2014).

CHAPTER 7. AGES OF DELUGE AND DROUGHT

1. Werner, *Myths and Legends of China,* 56.
2. Wilkins, *Mysteries of Ancient South America,* 31.
3. "J Harlen Bretz," Wikipedia, http://en.wikipedia.org/wiki/J_Harlen_Bretz (accessed May 31, 2014).
4. Li et al., "Synchronizing a Sea-Level Jump."

5. O'Riordan, "Coral Reef."

6. Marshall et al., "Late Pleistocene and Holocene Drought Events."

7. Scotsman, "Ancient Egypt Was Destroyed by Drought."

8. "List of Dynasties," note 2, on "granaries," California Institute for Ancient Studies, www.specialtyinterests.net/dyn3.html (accessed May 31, 2014).

9. Alan Winston [Jimmy Dunn], "The Mortuary Temple, Serdab, Northern Courtyard and the West Mounds of the Step Pyramid of Djoser at Saqqara, Egypt," Tour Egypt, www.touregypt.net/featurestories/dsteppyramid3.htm (accessed May 31, 2014).

10. Lauer, *Saqqara*, 98.

11. Bard, *Encyclopedia of the Archaeology of Ancient Egypt*, 864.

12. Ibid., 129.

13. Petrie, *Pyramids and Temples*, 80–82.

14. Howard Vyse, *Operations*, 206–7.

15. Dave Roberts, "Scientist Explains Likely Cause of Grain Elevator Explosions," KWCH, http://articles.kwch.com/2012-02-02/grain-dust_31019435 (accessed May 31, 2014).

16. Hancock, *Fingerprints of the Gods*, 363.

17. Hassan, *Sphinx*, 222–24.

18. John Anthony West, private e-mail to Scott Creighton.

19. W. Woelfli and W. Baltensperger, "On the Change of Latitude of Arctic East Siberia at the End of the Pleistocene," Cornell University Library, http://arxiv.org/abs/0704.2489 (accessed May 30, 2014).

20. W. Woelfli and W. Baltensperger, "Traditions Connected with the Pole Shift Model," Cornell University Library, http://arxiv.org/abs/1009.5078 (accessed May 30, 2014).

21. Creighton and Osborn, *Giza Prophecy*, 243–48.

22. Dilbeck, "Opening the Gates of Paradise."

23. Ibid.

CHAPTER 8. FLYING STONES

1. Lehner, *Complete Pyramids*, 215.

2. Ibid., 211.

CHAPTER 9. PROJECT OSIRIS

1. Plato, *Timaeus.*
2. Belzoni, *Narrative of the Operations,* 275.
3. Nichols, "Herodotus and Diodorus Verified by Belzoni," 315.
4. Lehner, *Complete Pyramids,* 124.
5. Milly Farrell, acting curator, Royal College of Surgeons, London, private e-mail to Scott Creighton.
6. Tooley, "Osiris Bricks," 171–72.
7. Budge, *The Egyptian Book of the Dead,* li.
8. Griffiths, *Origins of Osiris,* 66–67.

CHAPTER 10. JOURNEY'S END

1. Elizabeth Kaye McCall, "Saving the Secrets of the Sands: Zahi A. Hawass," Guardian's Egypt, www.guardians.net/hawass/article1a.htm (accessed May 31, 2014).
2. Budge, *The Book of the Dead,* 59–60.

Bibliography

Allen, James P. *The Ancient Egyptian Pyramid Texts*. Atlanta, Ga.: Society of Biblical Literature, 2005.

Assmann, Jan. *The Mind of Egypt: History and Meaning in the Time of the Pharaohs*. Bonn: Metropolitan Books, 2002.

Bard, Kathryn A. *Encyclopedia of the Archaeology of Ancient Egypt*. New York: Routledge, 1999.

———. *An Introduction to the Archaeology of Ancient Egypt*. Hoboken, N.J.: Wiley-Blackwell, 2007.

Bauval, Robert, and Adrian Gilbert. *The Orion Mystery*. London: William Heinemann Ltd., 1994.

Belzoni, Giovanni B. *Narrative of the Operations and Recent Discoveries within the Pyramids, Temples, Tombs, and Excavations, in Egypt and Nubia*. London: John Murray, 1820.

Budge, E. A. Wallis. *The Book of the Dead—The Papyrus of Ani in the British Museum*. 1895. Reprint, Cosimo Classics, 2010.

———. *From Fetish to God in Ancient Egypt*. Oxford University Press, 1934.

———. *Legends of the Gods: The Egyptian Texts*. London: Kegan Paul, Trench and Trübner & Co. Ltd, 1912.

Cattane, Valentina. "Egyptian Archeologists Comment on Carbon Dating." *Egypt Independent,* August 7, 2010. www.egyptindependent.com/news/egyptian-archeologists-comment-carbon-dating. Accessed May 30, 2014.

Cayce, Edgar. *Edgar Cayce's Egypt: Psychic Revelations on the Most Fascinating Civilization Ever Known*. Virginia Beach, Va.: A.R.E. Press, 2004.

Creighton, Scott, and Gary Osborn. *The Giza Prophecy*. Rochester, Vt.: Bear & Company, 2012.

Dilbeck, Gwynne Ann, "Opening the Gates of Paradise: Function and the Iconographical Program of Ghiberti's Bronze Door." Dissertation, University of Iowa, 2011. http://ir.uiowa.edu/etd/2691. Accessed August 8, 2014.

Doreal, trans. *The Emerald Tablets of Thoth-the-Atlantean*. Indianapolis, Ind.: Dog Ear Publishing, 2002.

Edwards, Sir I. E. S. *The Pyramids of Egypt*. New York: Penguin Books, 1947.

Evans, Lorraine. *Kingdom of the Ark*. London: Simon & Schuster U.K. Ltd., 2000.

Great Britain House of Commons. *Journals of the House of Commons, Vol. 62*. London: HM Stationery Office, 1807.

Griffiths, John G. *The Origins of Osiris and His Cult*. Boston: Brill, 1980.

Hancock, Graham. *Fingerprints of the Gods*. Mandarin Paperbacks, 1996.

Hassan, Selim. *The Sphinx: Its History in the Light of Recent Excavations*. Government Press, 1949.

Higgins, Frank C. *Ancient Freemasonry: An Introduction to Masonic Archeology*. New York: Kessinger Publishing, 1919.

Honore, Carl. *The Slow Fix*. New York, London, Toronto: Alfred A. Knopf, 2013.

James, Peter. *Centuries of Darkness*. New Brunswick, N.J.: Rutgers University Press, 1993.

Lauer, J. P. *Saqqara: The Royal Cemetery of Memphis; Excavations and Discoveries since 1850*. London: Thames & Hudson Ltd., 1976.

Lawton, Ian, and Chris Ogilvie-Herald. *Giza: The Truth*. London: Virgin Books, 2002.

Lehner, Mark. *The Complete Pyramids*. London: Thames & Hudson, 1997.

Lepre, J. P. *The Egyptian Pyramids: A Comprehensive, Illustrated Reference*. Jefferson, N.C.: McFarland, 2006.

Li, Yong-Xiang, Torbjörn E. Törnqvist, Johanna M. Nevitt, and Barry Kohl. "Synchronizing a Sea-Level Jump, Final Lake Agassiz Drainage, and Abrupt Cooling 8200 Years Ago." *Earth and Planetary Science Letters* 315–16 (January 15, 2012): 41–50.

Marshall, Michael H., Henry F. Lamb, Dei Huws, et al. "Late Pleistocene and Holocene Drought Events at Lake Tana, the Source of the Blue

Nile." *Global and Planetary Change* 78, no. 3–4 (August–September 2011): 147–61.

Massey, Gerald. *Gerald Massey's Lectures*. Whitefish, Mont.: Kessinger Publishing, 1992.

Murtadi, Ibn Gaphiphus. *The Egyptian History*. Translated by John Davies. London: Robert Battersby, 1672.

Naydler, Jeremy. *Temple of the Cosmos: The Ancient Egyptian Experience of the Sacred*. Rochester, Vt.: Inner Traditions International, 1996.

Nichols, John. *The Gentleman's Magazine and Historical Chronicle* 92, part 2, 1822.

O'Riordan, Bernard. "Coral Reef Clue to Fast Sea Rise." *Guardian*, February 24, 2005. www.theguardian.com/world/2005/feb/24/australia .environment. Accessed May 31, 2014.

Petrie, William Matthew Flinders. *The Pyramids and Temples of Gizeh*. London: Field and Tuer, 1883.

Picknett, Lynn, and Clive Prince. *The Sion Revelation*. New York: Time Warner, 2006.

Plato. *Timaeus and Critias*. Translated by Benjamin Jowett. Digireads.com Publishing, 2009.

Plutarch. *Moralia Vol V: Isis and Osiris*. Translated by Frank Cole Babbit. Cambridge, Mass.: Harvard University Press, 1989.

Schoedler, Friedrich. *The Book of Nature: An Elementary Introduction to the Sciences of Physics, Astronomy, Chemistry, Mineralogy, Geology, Botany, Zoology, and Physiology*. Translated by Henry Medlock. Philadelphia: Blanchard & Lea, 1853.

"Ancient Egypt Was Destroyed by Drought, Discover Scottish Experts." *Scotsman*. August 2, 2011. www.scotsman.com/news/ancient-egypt-was -destroyed-by-drought-discover-scottish-experts-1-1777592. Accessed May 31, 2014.

Sitchin, Zecharia. *Journeys to the Mythical Past*. Rochester, Vt.: Bear & Co, 2007.

Smyth, Charles Piazzi. *Our Inheritance in the Great Pyramid*. London: W. Isbister & Co, 1874.

Staple, Philip. *Journals of the House of Commons* 62 (1807): 680.

Strouhal, Evzen. *Life of the Ancient Egyptians*. University of Oklahoma Press, 1992.

Thorne, R. G. *The History of Parliament: The House of Commons; 1790–1820.* Vol. 1, Survey. London: Secker & Warburg, 1986.

Tooley, Angela M. J., "Osiris Bricks." *Journal of Egyptian Archaeology* 82 (1996): 167–79.

Vyse, Richard W. H. *Operations Carried on at the Pyramids of Gizeh.* Vol. 1 and II. London: James Fraser, 1840.

———. Private Journal. 1837. Aylesbury: Centre for Buckinghamshire Studies.

Werner, E. T. C. *Myths and Legends of China.* Mineola, N.Y.: Dover Publications, 1994.

Wilkins , Harold T. *Mysteries of Ancient South America.* London: Forgotten Books, 2012.

Zivie-Coche, Christiane. *Sphinx: History of a Monument.* 1997 Reprint. Ithaca, N.Y.: Cornell University Press, 2002.

Index

Page numbers in *italic* refer to illustrations.

BOOKS OF RELATED INTEREST

The Giza Prophecy
The Orion Code and the Secret Teachings of the Pyramids
by Scott Creighton and Gary Osborn
Foreword by Graham Hancock

Esoteric Egypt
The Sacred Science of the Land of Khem
by J. S. Gordon

Land of the Fallen Star Gods
The Celestial Origins of Ancient Egypt
by J. S. Gordon

The Giza Power Plant
Technologies of Ancient Egypt
by Christopher Dunn

Lost Technologies of Ancient Egypt
Advanced Engineering in the Temples of the Pharaohs
by Christopher Dunn

Black Genesis
The Prehistoric Origins of Ancient Egypt
by Robert Bauval and Thomas Brophy, Ph.D.

Ancient Egypt 39,000 BCE
The History, Technology, and Philosophy of Civilization X
by Edward F. Malkowski

Return of the Golden Age
Ancient History and the Key to Our Collective Future
by Edward F. Malkowski

INNER TRADITIONS • BEAR & COMPANY
P.O. Box 388
Rochester, VT 05767
1-800-246-8648
www.InnerTraditions.com

Or contact your local bookseller